Praise for 3

Sometimes I'm asked to give my all-time favorite book on evangelism. My answer? The book of Acts. Read the book of Acts and try to justify the institutional, formulaic Christianity we see so often today. Instead, when you read The Acts you read about a movement—a movement of gospel advances that has changed the whole world. My dear friend Dr. Doug Munton has given you a wonderful resource in this devotional that takes you through The Acts in a month's time. Read the Word, then read Doug's words about the Word and be changed—be part of a movement!

—Dr. Alvin L. Reid
Professor of Evangelism and
Student Ministry/Bailey Smith Chair of Evangelism,
Southeastern Baptist Theological Seminary, Wake Forest, NC
Author, *As You Go: Creating a Missional Culture of Gospel-Centered Students*, and *Firefall 2.0: How God Has Shaped History Through Revivals*

In 30 Days to Acts, Dr. Doug Munton has provided us with a tremendous devotional resource. This book, designed to be read in just one month, will help you understand the book of Acts like never before, while reminding you that God's mission for the church remains your mission in the church—to make disciples!

—Dr. Bill Curtis
Senior Pastor, Cornerstone Baptist Church, Darlington, SC
Award-Winning Author, *Engaging Exposition*, *30 Days to James*, and *Exalting Jesus in Micah*

In a pressure packed world, there is a never-ending struggle to stay on track as Christians. God wants us to enjoy a life of intimacy with Him and to be fully engaged in missional living as His church—but we all need help. That help can be found in Doug Munton's new book, *30 Days to Acts*. In this book, Doug explores the lives of first century Christ-followers, who shared the hope of the Gospel in a pressure packed world of their own. From church leaders like Paul, to ordinary people like Cornelius, Doug guides us through their stories, inspiring us along the way. I believe you will find that this one-month excursion into the Book of Acts will not only inspire you but also equip you to get on track, and stay on track, as you live to glorify our great Savior!

—Dr. Tim Dowdy
Senior Pastor, Eagles Landing First Baptist Church, McDonough, GA
Author, *Don't Forget to Dream*

The church must advance the gospel—it is the only source of hope for the world. Dr. Doug Munton has given us a very helpful study in a very important book. He helps us find our place in God's ongoing story of redemption. This "30-Day" study is exactly what my church members need for their personal devotions and small group Bible studies.

—Dr. Dwayne Milioni
Senior Pastor, Open Door Baptist Church, Raleigh, NC
Co-Founder, The Pillar Church Planting Network

In *30 Days to Acts,* Dr. Doug Munton writes with clarity and grace, taking his readers on an exciting journey into the heart of the gospel, the explosive expansion of the early church, and the praxis of missional living. As I read Dr. Munton's insightful expositions, I was convicted by the Holy Spirit to live each day of my life seeking to "turn the world upside down," just as the earliest followers of Jesus did!

—Dr. Stephen Rummage
Senior Pastor, Bell Shoals Baptist Church, Brandon, FL
Award-winning Author, *Engaging Exposition* and
Planning your Preaching

Do you want to live as a vital Christian today? Then read this book. Dr. Doug Munton takes you on a journey exploring the movement of God in the early church, and shows you how to be a catalyst for the movement of God today. He will lead you on a 30-day journey through the Book of Acts that teaches you how to be used of the Holy Spirit spreading God's Kingdom in the world!

—Dr. Greg Faulls
Senior Pastor, Bellevue Baptist Church, Owensboro, KY
Author, *From Dust to Destiny*

The Book of Acts tells of the early days of the church, when the disciples of Jesus were figuring out what it meant to be Christ followers. There was no template to follow. The Book of Acts tells us how those early followers of Jesus succeeded and failed, suffered and prospered, worshiped and witnessed. In *30 Days to Acts*, Dr. Doug Munton has captured the soul of the Book of Acts. He reveals the challenge of looking back to anchor our lives to Christ while actually living in our own modern world. Doug's book will encourage you to stand in the life-changing power of Jesus' resurrection, while sharing His life-changing message with our modern world.

—Dr. Chet Roden
Professor of Old Testament, Liberty School of Divinity
Author, *30 Days to Genesis*

There is a huge difference between reading your Bible and understanding your Bible. Many Christians recognize this truth but struggle with how to bridge the gap between the two. Thankfully help has arrived. In *30 Days to Acts*, Dr. Doug Munton has provided a valuable resource to help you both read your Bible AND understand your Bible. Guiding you through Luke's account of the early days of the New Testament church, Dr. Munton explains the Book of Acts by offering personal insights, practical applications, and life-changing truths. Additionally, he provides daily, text-driven prayer guides that will challenge you to live as a co-laborer for the gospel in God's church. If you're looking for a resource to take the place of your daily Bible reading, then *30 Days to Acts* is not for you. But, if you're looking for a resource that will take your daily Bible reading to a whole new level, then open your Bible, open this book, and prepare to be challenged and blessed. After walking through *30 Days to Acts*, you will not only have read your Bible, but you will also understand what you've read and how it can change your life!

—Dr. Mark Howell
Senior Pastor, First Baptist Church, Daytona, FL
Author, *Exalting Jesus in 1 & 2 Thessalonians*

30 DAYS TO
ACTS

30 Days to Acts

A Devotional Commentary

Doug Munton

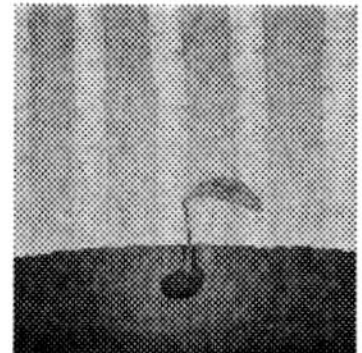

Seed Publishing Group, LLC
Timmonsville, South Carolina

30 Days to Acts: A Devotional Commentary

Published by:
Seed Publishing Group
2570 Double C Farm Ln
Timmonsville, SC 29161
seed-publishing-group.com

Edited by:
Bill Curtis, Ph.D.
Dwayne Milioni, Ph.D.

To order additional copies of this resource visit www.seed-publishing-group.com.

Library of Congress Control Number: 2015915203

ISBN-13: 978-0-9968412-1-4

1 2 3 4 5 6 7 8 9 10

Printed in the United States of America

Dedication

I am well into my twentieth year as the pastor of First Baptist Church of O'Fallon, Illinois and I am more thankful than ever for the people of that great church. We have witnessed and discipled together. We have laughed and wept together. We have seen hundreds of new people come and, often due to new Air Force assignments, we have seen hundreds leave to go to the ends of the earth. It has been exciting, exhilarating, scary and awesome. In other words, it has often felt like the book of Acts.

My journey is shared with my wife, Vickie, who is my therapist, counselor, encourager and dearest friend. She has proofed, suggested and even cajoled. She has been a tremendous help as has the rest of my family. My four kids and their spouses are strong in faith and a joy to my heart. My five grandchildren slow my progress in the happiest of ways. As much as I enjoyed writing this book, it cannot compare to the joy of wrestling matches with my young grandchildren!

Contents

Contents

Foreword

Since my early days as a new believer, I have been fascinated by the book of Acts - the sheer wonder of this audacious story of a small group of nobodies who transformed culture and history by the power of the gospel. But even more than the history of this story, I am amazed by the fact that the Bible calls us to be IN the story! The book of Acts is an unfinished book. Read the last chapter – no one ends a story like this unless there is more to be written. We are writing the last chapters of the book of Acts now!

We get to be a part of finishing the history of the church on this earth. What an incredibly important journey it is to walk through the book of Acts and then see it come alive in our own lives. I know of no one better to take us on this journey than Doug Munton. Doug is my best friend. I have watched him live out his faith for years with a boldness and love that mirrors the book of Acts. He has seen incredible church growth like that in the book of Acts. He has lived through the highs and lows of life with Jesus and life with the people of God just as we see in the book of Acts. He has seen revival as we have learned to pray for it in the book of Acts. His words will bring the Word of God to life in you as you read them.

Every year, at least once, I go to the persecuted church. I hope the ministry I do there is helpful to these precious people, but honestly, I go for a fairly selfish reason: I NEED to be there. I need to see the book of Acts lived out, and we see that most clearly in the persecuted church. One person that I met there years ago, named Constantine, had gone through horrible suffering. One day I asked him,

Foreword

"Brother Constantine, how did you endure this? What is your secret? How did you face such suffering?" He looked at me with surprise, almost in shock and said, "Don't you know?" I said, "I don't think I do." His reply was, "Jesus is enough! The Word of God is enough. Tell everyone that you speak to that Jesus is enough. The Word of God is enough!" I have never forgotten his words. He didn't have a list of 10 ways to endure suffering or how to live with authentic faith in a messed up world. He just knew personally that Jesus and his Word were enough. *30 Days to Acts* will help you to live in the incredible, mysterious, and wonderful truth that Jesus and his Word are enough. The thirty days you spend in this book will prepare you to play your part in finishing the story of the book of Acts.

—Dr. John Avant

Preface

The book of Acts is exciting and a bit intimidating. One cannot help but be thrilled at the miraculous events, the bold witness and the explosive growth that is written about in Acts. But it can be intimidating to read of faith that seems so much deeper and witness that seems so much bolder than what one sees in the life of the average church and Christian today.

Rather than intimidation from the book, I want to suggest that we desire imitation of the book. Let's ask the Lord to help us to learn all we can from this great book of the Bible so that we can discover the same passion and power that we see in the early church. Let's ask the Lord to make us bold and to fill us with faith and to use us in powerful ways. Let's follow the example of Spirit-filled men like Peter, Paul and Barnabas. Let's ask the Lord to give our churches life like the church at Antioch or discernment like the church at Berea. The Lord gives us the book of Acts as an example of what our lives and churches can be like when we are filled with the Holy Spirit and walking by faith.

Let me suggest some things in connection with reading *30 Days to Acts*. First, read it with someone else, or better yet, with a group of people. Reading it with a Bible study group or a Sunday School class or others will help you get the most out of it. As you discuss together what God is teaching you, there will be mutual benefit and encouragement. Perhaps your entire church could go through these 30 days together.

Second, read the verses for the day before reading the devotional words that follow. Read the verses carefully and prayerfully and allow those words to sink into your soul. Then read the focal verse and the devotional words that follow.

Also, read one chapter per day. Perhaps the "30 Days" part of the title already clued you in to that idea. Instead of reading through the entire book, read a chapter each day. This will help you to develop the healthy pattern of a daily devotional time and it will allow the words of each day to sink in a bit.

I am praying for you. I am praying that every person who reads *30 Days to Acts* will experience the presence and the power of the Holy Spirit in his or her own life. As you read this book, I am praying God will open your heart to what he wants to do in your life and through your life. I'm praying that reading this book will awaken a hunger in your heart for God to work in your life as he did in the lives of the men and women of the early church.

Ask him to guide you on this journey and to do something so great in your heart that you know it is from him. I pray God blesses the next 30 days of your life in a special way!

One more thing . . . This book is part of a larger series of books that is being developed by Seed Publishing Group; it is called *30 Days to the Bible*. Each year, several new books will be added to this series until all the books of the Bible have been covered. Renowned scholars and pastors from around the country will be writing books for this exciting, new series. So, if you like *30 Days to Acts*, keep your eyes open for the next books in the series: *30 Days to James, 30 Days to Genesis, 30 Days to the Parables, 30 Days to John*, and *30 Days to Colossians*!

Finally, Seed Publishing Group is an indie publisher committed to bringing great resources to both individual Christians and the local church (please visit them at www.seed-publishing-group.com). As part of that commitment, they are partners with The Pillar Network for church planting (www.thepillarnetwork.com). $1 from each sale of *30 Days to Acts* goes directly to church plants throughout North America. Thank you for purchasing *30 Days to Acts,* and thank you for investing in church planting!

The Big Plan

Acts 1:1-8

You will receive power when the Holy Spirit has come upon you, and you will be my witnesses in Jerusalem and in all Judea and Samaria, and to the end of the earth.
Act 1:8

The book of Acts begins with God's big plan to impact the world with the message of the gospel. So what is this great plan for changing the world? The answer is shockingly simple. God's plan is to have people like us take the message of the gospel to others. It seems like God's plan should be grander or more dramatic. But God in heaven has chosen to use people like you and me to spread the message of his love. He uses fishermen, tax collectors, bankers, housewives, students and ditch diggers. God wants to use you, if you know him as your Savior, as the means by which others hear the message of his love. We are to be "witnesses," verse eight tells us.

Maybe you are a bit intimidated by God's big plan to use you as a witness. It seems a bit overwhelming and kind of scary. You may wonder, "Can God really use me?" But let me assure you that God is able to use you in this task. And he reminds us of some important lessons that encourage us to participate in his plan. There are three specific things about this big plan of God's that I want you to note.

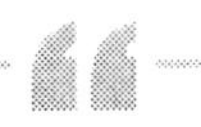

God's plan is to have people like us take the message of the gospel to others.

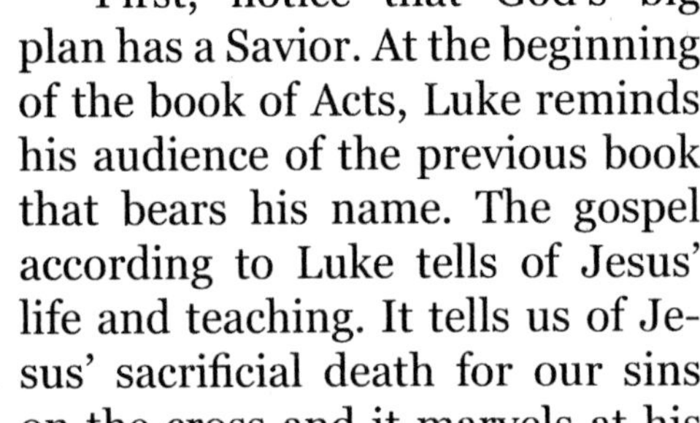

First, notice that God's big plan has a Savior. At the beginning of the book of Acts, Luke reminds his audience of the previous book that bears his name. The gospel according to Luke tells of Jesus' life and teaching. It tells us of Jesus' sacrificial death for our sins on the cross and it marvels at his resurrection from the dead. Luke notes in Acts 1:3 that Jesus "presented himself alive to them after his suffering by many convincing proofs." In other words, Jesus provided us with evidence that he was more than just a man. He was and is God who became a man, our Savior and our hope.

We ought never to forget that God's big plan is centered on the Savior. It isn't primarily about our strategies, cleverness, programs or church buildings. The plan is centered on the person of our Savior. Jesus is at the center of the plan. He is the only one who can forgive sins. He is the only one who can change hearts. He is the only one who can offer eternal life. It is all about him. He is the key, not us. The focus of an effective witness is Jesus and his message.

Second, note that God's big plan has a Spirit. In verses four and five, Jesus told his disciples to stay in Jerusalem where they would be "baptized with the Holy Spirit." Though Jesus would soon ascend back into heaven, he did not leave his followers without God's presence. The Holy Spirit was sent to indwell the life of every believer.

Note how verse eight puts it. "You will receive power when the Holy Spirit has come upon you." In the Holy Spirit, the believer has the presence and the power of God in his or her life. The word translated "power" is the word that we use for dynamite. It is a description of God's great ability to do his work through our lives.

God is not sending you to participate in this big plan on your own. You are empowered by his Spirit who guides you, encourages you and enables you. This plan is certainly too big for you or me, but it isn't too big for the Holy Spirit who lives in us. He gives us the power and strength to accomplish this task of witnessing to the world. And the believer doesn't face this challenging responsibility alone. The Holy Spirit is present with us every step of the way.

The third thing I want you to recognize is that God's big plan has a strategy. We can break God's game plan down into parts. The strategy is for us to be witnesses "in Jerusalem and in all Judea and Samaria, and to the end of the earth."

Some have suggested that we consider these locations as four components to an overall strategy. Jerusalem was local. It was where the disciples were at the moment. We are to witness where we are, in our home, job site, or school. Judea was the region that was like Jerusalem. It crossed no cultural barriers, just geographical ones. We are to witness to others who are like us. We can witness to extended family, those who live in our neighborhoods and those beyond.

Notice, however, that the areas expand beyond that. Samaria was a different cultural area than Judea. Jesus told his followers to cross these cultural divides with the message of the gospel. There were some cultural differences between the Jews and the Samaritans. Jesus told them to witness anyway. There was some lingering hostility between the groups. Jesus told them to witness anyway. The message of the gospel is not just for those who have grown up like us.

Then, the plan gets exponentially bigger. Jesus told his followers to witness "to the end of the earth." Is that big enough for you? God's plan is for people like you and me to witness of his grace, mercy, and love to those near and far--those like us and those different from us. I told you this was a big plan!

The focus of an effective witness is Jesus and his message.

God in heaven wants to involve you in his huge plan for this world. God wants to use you to make a difference on this planet by sharing the message of the gospel. Think of this. God will use your knowledge of the gospel, your experience of salvation, and even your location on this globe as a means by which you can have an impact that lasts for eternity.

This plan is so big that only God can empower it, yet it is so personal that you can participate in it. If you know Christ as Savior, God invites you to join him in this exciting journey of faith by living as a witness for him. Join God in his great plan to take the life-changing message of the love of Jesus everywhere.

Food for Thought

God wants to use you as a witness. He wants you involved in this great work of sharing the message of the gospel with others. And, if you know Christ as your Savior, he has empowered you with the Holy Spirit who will enable you to do this great work. What is it that makes you fearful of being a witness? Is it lack of knowledge? Is it fear of what others might think about you? Have you forgotten how important this task is to God? God will use you if you are willing to be used by him.

Faith in Action

Open your heart and mind to those around you who need to hear the message of the gospel today. Consider those in your family or among your acquaintances who need to hear this message. Look for opportunities to share your faith. Pray with boldness and ask for more boldness. Perhaps there is a missionary who needs your prayers and support. God might even want you to participate in a mission trip.

Prayer

Ask God to give you an awareness of the spiritual needs of those around you. Ask him to provide opportunities for you to share your faith and for the wisdom to see and seize those opportunities. Ask him to help you overcome any fears or doubts you might have and to trust him to help you in sharing your faith with others. Ask him to give you boldness as you share the love of God with others.

Don't Just Stand There

Acts 1:9-14

Men of Galilee, why do you stand looking into heaven? This Jesus, who was taken up from you into heaven, will come in the same way as you saw him go into heaven.
Acts 1:11

It must have been quite a sight—Jesus ascending into heaven while the disciples looked on in amazement and wonder. Don't you wish you could have been there? Wouldn't you like to have watched as Jesus disappeared into the clouds? It must have been amazing. Like the disciples, we would have wanted to continue gazing into the heavens allowing the wonder of the moment to sink in. We would have stood there with mouths wide open and eyes blinking in the sun, yet unable to turn away.

The Billy Graham museum on the campus of my alma mater, Wheaton College, captures some of the essence of this moment. After meandering through the museum that chronicles the history of evangelists through the ages, focusing on the ministry of Billy Graham, one is led through a corridor with twists and turns. The corridor leads one on a journey through the meaning of the cross. One is reminded of the sacrifice made by our Savior, and there is a palpable sadness in the air as the corridor leads

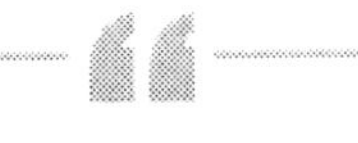

At some point, we must move from the wonder of one day to the responsibilities of this day.

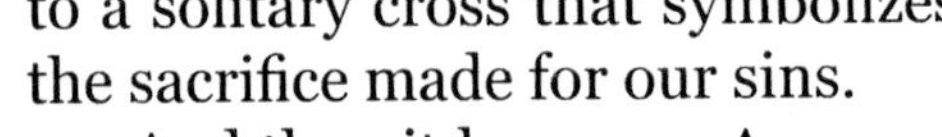

to a solitary cross that symbolizes the sacrifice made for our sins.

And then it happens. A corner is turned. The somber background music of the cross is replaced by what sounds like distant angels. The next step reveals a stunning room. It is filled with light and glass and the 3D imagery of clouds all around. It reminds one of resurrection, heaven, and joy. It must have been something of what the disciples felt as Jesus ascended to heaven in the clouds: beauty and joy and glory. When I take people through the museum for the first time, I always try to stand behind them as they enter that room. I love to watch their expression turn from being serious and sober to happiness and amazement.

People usually linger in that room. One doesn't want to leave too quickly. It is such a hopeful place and reminds one of a distant home they have never seen, but to which they long to return. When one does finally leave, carved into the wall are these words, "Men of Galilee, why do you stand looking into heaven? This Jesus, who was taken up from you into heaven, will come in the same way as you saw him go into heaven." At some point, we must stop looking into the air and watching for the Lord to return; we must get busy serving Christ in the here and now. We must move from the wonder of one day to the responsibilities of this day.

This passage is a great reminder that we can serve Christ effectively in the "in between." These days between the resurrection of Christ and the return of Christ are important days. The angels call us back to our need to serve the Lord during our limited days until Christ returns. We are called by our Lord to serve him effectively and faithfully in the here and now. Our Bible verses remind us of three reasons why we can serve Christ effectively in these days.

One reason we can serve Christ effectively is because Christ is returning. The ascension of the Lord is tied closely to the return of the Lord. The angels reminded the skyward-gazing disciples that Jesus was going to return just as he had ascended. This is a reminder to us that Jesus is returning and that we have responsibilities in the meantime.

I am very thankful that those who know Christ as Savior are promised heaven one day. But we aren't in heaven yet. (Your streets aren't paved with gold are they?) So, we have responsibilities to serve the Lord right now.

Knowing that the Lord is returning is motivation for my service. I know that he can return at any time and that I am to be busy serving him in the limited time I have in this life. But knowing the Lord is returning isn't just motivation for me, it also encourages me. I am so thankful to know that we are not abandoned in this life. He didn't just leave us. The Lord will return to claim his own.

A second reason we can serve Christ effectively is because the Holy Spirit is filling us. Verse 12 tells us that the disciples listened to the angels' message and then returned to Jerusalem. Why did they go to Jerusalem? Because Jesus, before ascending into heaven, told them to remain in Jerusalem and wait for the promise the Father had for them—the filling of the Holy Spirit (see Acts 1:4-5).

We can serve the Lord effectively because we can be filled with the presence and the power of the Holy Spirit. God, who is and always has been Father, Son, and Holy Spirit—one God with three ways of being—lives in the life of believers. The Holy Spirit empowers us for service. He guides us into God's will. He enables us to make an impact in the world for God's glory. How awesome to think that God lives in our lives to empower us for all he wants to do for us and through us. We are not alone. We have God's strength and God's power to accomplish all he wants for us.

God wants to move his followers from observation to action.

A third reason we can serve Christ effectively is because God's people are praying. I love what happened next. Verse 14 says, "All these with one accord were devoting themselves to prayer." Prayer is powerful. These men and women gathered together to earnestly pray. They were "devoting" themselves to this great endeavor.

When God is working we typically discover that somewhere in the background people are praying. Prayer is seeking the Lord for his direction, pouring out our needs and concerns before him, and accessing God's strength for the need at hand. Prayer is powerful.

Notice that the text says they were praying "with one accord." That is, they were all seeking the same thing from the same Lord for the same purpose. They were seeking God's will and not their own. We have many differences as believers. We have different backgrounds, perspectives, talents, and gifts. What is it that draws us together? We are drawn together in one accord when we all lay aside our own desires and desire God's perfect will.

God wants to move his followers from observation to action. We are not merely spectators watching God at work. We are to be participants who are actively engaged in God's exciting work. And, we don't just remember what God has done in the past. We join God in the work that he is doing in the present while anticipating what he is going to do in the future.

Food for Thought

God wants you to be involved in his life changing work. While we remember all that he has done for us in the past, we are to live actively engaged in the present as we prepare for God's culminating work in the future. We aren't to just stand around gazing at the heavens. God wants us fully participating in his great work.

Faith in Action

Identify ways you can get engaged in the work God is doing in the world here and now. Use your gifts, talents, and resources to make a difference. Look for opportunities in your church to participate in his work. Start with a serious commitment to prayer as you seek God's direction and power. If you don't already do this, begin a regular time with God each day in his word and in prayer.

Prayer

Ask the Lord to use you in the world right now. Ask him to help you get serious about prayer and active service. Ask the Lord to provide opportunities now as you anticipate his return in the future.

Filled with the Holy Spirit

Acts 2:1-21

And all were amazed and perplexed, saying to one another, "What does this mean?"
Acts 2:12

"Amazed and perplexed." That was the response of the people to the work of the Holy Spirit 2,000 years ago. Not much has changed. People are still amazed and perplexed at the work of the Holy Spirit today. I am okay with the "amazed" part. We ought to be amazed at the work of the Holy Spirit. But perhaps we should do something about the "perplexed" part.

It had been a whirlwind of events. First, there was the arrest of Jesus, the mockery of a trial, and the soul-searing crucifixion of the Lord. That was followed by the shocking rumor, then the full confirmation of the resurrection of Jesus from the dead. But the joy of Jesus' resurrected presence was tempered when he ascended into heaven one beautiful day. And now, gathered together in Jerusalem, the disciples were to experience one more spectacular event orchestrated by the power of the great God who made the universe.

As they huddled together in a house in Jerusalem on the day of Pentecost, the early Christians experienced

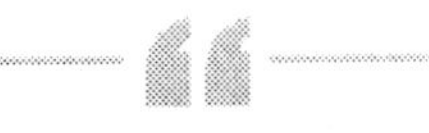

The Holy Spirit gives us his presence to fulfill God's purpose in our lives.

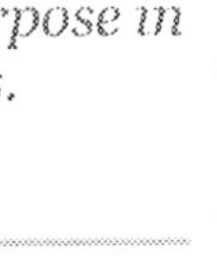

an amazing thing. There was a loud noise that sounded like a mighty rushing wind. Perhaps it was like the sound before a terrific thunderstorm or a powerful tornado. It was immediately followed by what appeared to be divided tongues of fire that rested on each of them. The Bible tells us in Acts 2:4 that they were all filled with the Holy Spirit, and they began to speak, by the power of the Holy Spirit, in languages they had never learned.

This passage teaches us three important lessons that reveal who the Holy Spirit is and what he does in our lives. The first lesson we learn is that the Holy Spirit fills us with his presence. The first verses of Acts 2 tell us of the coming of the Holy Spirit to those first Christians. God the Holy Spirit lives in believers. We are not alone. The Holy Spirit gives us his presence to fulfill God's purpose in our lives.

As a child, my room could be a scary place at night. The shadows looked like monsters and the darkness like bad guys. But I found comfort in knowing that my dad was in the very next room. If any problems should arise, dad was nearby. Better than that, the Holy Spirit is present with me; not just in the next room, but in my very life. That's because he lives in the life of every believer. There are still scary places and difficult problems. But I am so glad to be assured of the presence of the Holy Spirit in my life. None of the monsters or bad guys of my life can stand against him. I will never face a problem too big for him to handle.

One can have the presence of the Holy Spirit without being filled with the Holy Spirit, of course. In fact, believers are commanded to "be filled with the Spirit" in recognition that we all have access to the Spirit but may not all be filled by him (see Eph 5:18).

Two obvious results of being filled with the Holy Spirit are full obedience and full surrender. By full obedience I mean that we have repented of our sins and are committed to holy living and following God's plan. Full surrender means we are seeking God's will and not our own. We are completely surrendered to God's purposes. You have access to the Holy Spirit right now if you know Jesus as Savior. But I want to urge you to be filled with the Holy Spirit. Fully surrender your life to God and fully obey him in every area of your life.

The second lesson this passage teaches us is that the Holy Spirit empowers us for his purpose. Gathered in Jerusalem that day were devout men from every nation who had come to worship at Pentecost. Hearing the rushing wind, they congregated near the place where the disciples had gathered. There they heard something amazing. Each of them heard the disciples proclaiming the mighty works of God. And, more amazing still, they each heard in their own native language.

The gospel was being proclaimed to them in their own language—their heart language. The Holy Spirit empowered the disciples to proclaim the good news of God in a language that each could understand. What an amazing event! Some even mistakenly thought it must be the result of drunkenness. But it was the result of something far more powerful than liquor. It was the evidence of the filling of the Holy Spirit.

Some say that the sign of being filled with the Holy Spirit is speaking in tongues. I respectfully disagree. I believe the Bible teaches that the sign of being filled with the Holy Spirit is boldness in witness. It isn't so much the miracles that distinguish the filling of the Spirit; it is the willingness of those filled by him to witness boldly of the saving work of the Lord Jesus.

The coming of the Holy Spirit is part of God's plan from eternity past.

The third lesson we learn from this passage is that the Holy

Spirit comes fulfilling prophecy. Acts 2:14-21 is the beginning of Peter's great sermon at Pentecost. There he points out that the coming of the Holy Spirit is part of God's plan from eternity past. He points to the prophet Joel who prophesied of the day of the coming of the Spirit. This prophecy was fulfilled at Pentecost.

It has always been God's plan to have his presence and power in the world in the person of the Holy Spirit. The great work of Pentecost was part of God's plan to send his presence into the lives of believers and his power into the midst of the world.

Food for Thought

You can be filled with the Holy Spirit today. God wants to make a difference in the world through your life now just as he did in the lives of the early believers at Pentecost. Surrender your life fully to him, and God the Holy Spirit will empower you to make a difference that will last for eternity. His work is truly amazing.

Faith in Action

Surrender your life fully to the Lord and ask him to fill you with the Holy Spirit. Obey fully every prompting of his leadership. Confess any known sins to the Lord who is faithful and just to forgive our sins. Obey him in every area of your life. Stop what he says to stop and begin what he says to begin. Surrender your will fully to his will.

Prayer

Ask the Lord to fill you with the Holy Spirit today. As you surrender to him and obey him, ask him to use you to make an impact in the world for his glory. Allow him to make the changes he wills to make in you. And then ask him to use you as a bold witness in the world of God's wonderful works.

What Shall We Do?

Acts 2:37-40

Now when they heard this they were cut to the heart, and said to Peter and the rest of the apostles, "Brothers, what shall we do?" Acts 2:37

A woman said to her pastor after his Sunday morning message, "Pastor, I want to thank you for your sermon today." The pastor replied piously, "Don't thank me. Thank God." "Oh," said the woman, "It wasn't *that* good!"

Acts 2 records the powerful message Peter preached at Pentecost. Filled and empowered by the Holy Spirit, his message was extraordinary. This was not just a message from a man; this was a message from God through a man. It was *that* good. Peter's message at Pentecost was a gospel message. He preached on the sinfulness of mankind and our need for a Savior. He told of Jesus who was both Lord and Christ by the declaration of the Father. He told of the cross of the Savior as the means of our salvation.

There is power in a gospel message. Note three things that happen when the message of the gospel is proclaimed through a preacher who is filled with the Holy Spirit. The first thing that happens through the preaching of the gospel is conviction. God used the message of the gospel that was preached by Peter to convict the gathered

There is pain in being cut to the heart, but painful surgery leads to genuine healing.

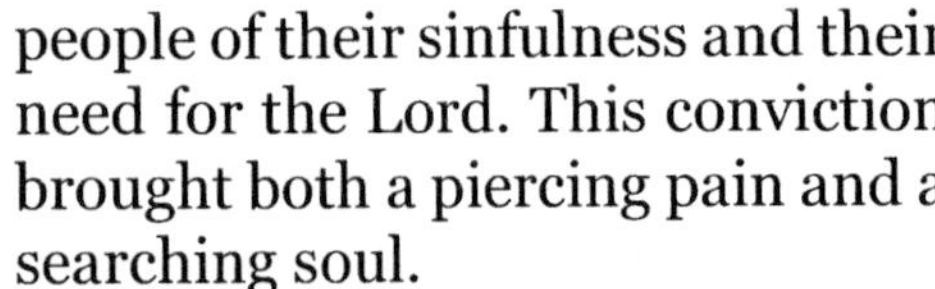

people of their sinfulness and their need for the Lord. This conviction brought both a piercing pain and a searching soul.

The Bible says in verse 37, "Now when they heard this they were cut to the heart." The imagery of a surgeon doing open-heart surgery is pictured here. The piercing pain of conviction was deep. I remember the pain of conviction that preceded my conversion. I was just a boy. I had not robbed any banks or committed any murders. I didn't yet know what larceny was, and there was no embezzlement of which I was aware. But I did know the pain of conviction. I knew what it was like to sin. I became painfully aware of my disobedience to my parents, my selfishness towards my friends, and my argumentative spirit with my brothers. Those sins were against God, and I had sinned against him. That guilt was painful, troubling, and helpful!

When we are cut to the heart we don't use these excuses. "My sins aren't so bad." "That sin isn't really my fault." "Sin is no big deal anyway." There is pain in being cut to the heart, but painful surgery leads to genuine healing.

Not only were the listeners to this sermon pierced, they began to search for an answer to their need and pain. They asked Peter and the other apostles, "Brothers, what shall we do?" Conviction led to a question, and because of the blood of Jesus Christ shed on the cross, that question had an answer.

A second thing that occurs through the preaching of the gospel is conversion. Not only did the sermon bring conviction, but also the sermon led to conversion. The people asked, "What shall we do?" Peter answered, "Repent." The word "repent" is a powerful word that has lost much of its meaning in our modern culture. We use the word when we feel sorry for something. We say, "That criminal was unrepentant," meaning that he didn't feel sorry at all for what he had done. The Greek word used in Acts 2 is "metanoia," which means far more than that. It refers to a mighty change of actions or attitudes. Repentance is more than feeling sorry for our sins. We can feel sorry without any change. Repentance is turning *from* sin and *to* the Lord.

Verse 38 continues, "Repent and be baptized every one of you in the name of Jesus Christ for the forgiveness of your sins." This verse has been controversial in religious circles. Is it saying, as some suggest, that one must be baptized in order to be saved? The word translated "for" is the Greek word "eis" which has two possible meanings here. It can mean "for," as in baptism is the act that must be performed to be saved. Or, it can mean "on the basis of," as in repentance is the saving act that precedes the act of baptism. Thankfully, the context provides the key to a proper interpretation.

Peter preached again about salvation in Acts 3. Verse 19 says, "Repent therefore, and turn back, that your sins may be blotted out." Here repentance is emphasized as the necessary act in salvation, and baptism is not even mentioned. Paul teaches the same thing in Eph 2:8-9, which states that salvation is by grace and not by works like baptism.

Despite the fact that baptism is not necessary for salvation, Peter mentions it in his response. Baptism is not an afterthought; it is an act of obedience and an act of great significance. Understating the role of baptism is as misleading as overstating it. Baptism, while not an act of salvation, is certainly an important act of obedience.

> *The gospel is always to be shared in the context of compassion.*

The third thing that happens through the preaching of the gospel is compassion. The gospel is always to be shared in the context of compassion. We are to care

The gospel message is powerful because it is more than the words of a preacher; it is truly God's sermon.

deeply about the people who hear this wonderful message.

Notice the persuasiveness of the sermon. "With many other words" Peter preached to them. He continued to "exhort" them. He deeply wanted them to come to faith. The text says, "He bore witness." That is, Peter shared the saving work of Jesus Christ in his own life. Also notice the call to commitment in the sermon. Peter concluded with the words, "Save yourselves from this crooked generation." He called them to commit to Christ then and there.

The gospel message is powerful because it is more than the words of a preacher; it is truly God's sermon.

Food for Thought

You can teach, preach, and witness with great confidence because the message of the gospel comes from God. God can use you to share that truth with others who may encounter the life-changing message of God's work of salvation.

Faith in Action

Do you ever find yourself afraid to share the gospel because you feel inadequate to change the other person's mind? Or maybe you don't think you will have the right words to explain it well? Take the time to read and recite Romans 1:16, "For I am not ashamed of the gospel, for it is the power of God for salvation to everyone who believes." There is power in the gospel message because it is the message from God. You can share it with the assurance that it is God's message, not yours.

Prayer

Ask the Lord to use you today to share the message of the gospel. Ask the Lord to open your eyes to opportunities to be a witness for Him. Ask God for the boldness that you need to speak his message to those who need to hear it.

The Passionate Church

Acts 2:41-47

And the Lord added to their number day by day those who were being saved.
Acts 2:47

As Billy Graham was preparing to speak at an upcoming crusade, it is said that a reporter tried to stir up some controversy. He referenced a theologian who had complained about the ministry of Billy Graham by saying that he was going to set back the work of the church by 200 years. What, the reporter asked, was Graham's response to this charge? Billy Graham's answer was amazing! He apologized to the theologian and everyone else within the Christian community. He said it wasn't his intention to set the church back 200 years; rather, it was his intention to set the church back 2,000 years!

If believers are to learn God's intention for the church of today, they should look back to the early church of 2,000 years ago. There we see a model and an example of what God wants in and from the church. The New Testament church gives us insights into the kind of church God wants for every culture and for every generation. While the details of musical style, cultural expression, and particular programs can change, the characteristics of what God

> *If believers are to learn God's intention for the church of today, they should look back to the early church of 2,000 years ago.*

wants a church to be remain the same in all places and at all times. We can learn much from the life and work of the early church.

The early church was a passionate church. Believers were passionate about the gospel and passionate about faith. They served with passion, sacrificed with passion, and lived with passion. Passion for the Lord and his work was obvious in everything they did. That kind of passion is needed among believers today. There is nothing wrong with some level of passion for sports, hobbies, or other things, but those things should pale in comparison with the greater work of the church. The church was passionate about the things that last and the things that matter.

There are four characteristics of this church recorded in Acts 2:41-47. Each of these characteristics springs from the passionate nature of the early church, and each of them should characterize the church of today.

First, a passionate church is a growing church. Verse 41 tells of 3,000 who heard the gospel and were baptized on that day of Pentecost. That was quite a day and quite a start for the early church! From the very beginning there were many people who were added to the church. The passion of the early church for reaching people was evidenced in its earliest days.

The passion of the early church to reach people is not merely evidenced by the response to Peter's sermon. It is also seen in the last sentence of chapter two. The Bible tells us in verse 47, "And the Lord added to their number day by day those who were being saved." Salvations were not limited to days like Pentecost or Sunday worship. "Day by day" people were coming to know the Lord as their Savior. Daily, the people shared the message of the gospel with those around them. The early church was passionate about sharing the gospel, and God blessed that passion.

Our churches today need to be passionate about reaching people and growing. The spiritual need of people leads us to passionate outreach; the love of Christ leads us to passionate outreach; the message of the gospel leads us to passionate outreach. And, the example of the early church leads us to reach out to people through our preaching and through our lives.

Ask God to give you and your church a passion for sharing the good news of God's love with others. The passion of the early church for the lost should inspire our churches to preach the message of the gospel publicly. And, it should lead us to share the message day by day with our neighbors, friends, coworkers, and classmates. We should desire that others experience the same salvation we have, and we should want our churches to grow and expand. The passion for sharing the message of the gospel that we see in the early church needs to be evident in the church of this generation. People need the bread of life, and we are beggars who have discovered that bread. A passionate church cares deeply about reaching those who haven't been reached and speaking to those who haven't heard.

Second, a passionate church is a learning church. Notice the description of those early believers in verse 42. "They devoted themselves to the apostles' teaching and the fellowship, to the breaking of bread and the prayers." They didn't just go through the motions of learning, they "devoted themselves." All who know the Lord should be passionate about learning. The early church set the example. They were devoted to four things as noted in the text.

They were devoted to the apostles' teaching. They wanted to know, understand, and put that teaching into practice. They were devoted to fellowship. Fellowship is a powerful New Testament word. It refers to the deep connections we have as believers.

The spiritual need of people leads us to passionate outreach.

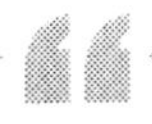

Learning to give cheerfully is the responsibility and the blessing of every believer.

We were saved for fellowship and connection with each other. This is why church membership and small groups are so valuable to believers.

Verse 42 tells us that the early church was devoted to the breaking of bread. This could refer to the Lord's Supper, to eating meals together, or, as I believe, to both. Their connection of fellowship was evidenced in their joining together in meals where they shared life together. And, it was born out of their connection with God as believers are reminded whenever we share the Lord's Supper together. Also, this early church was devoted to prayer. They prayed individually and together. They understood something of the power and the purpose of prayer, and it was a critical part of their lives.

Third, a passionate church is a giving church. Note the example of the giving nature of the early church in verses 44 and 45. Christians freely gave to help others who were in need. This was different than socialism where the government takes from some to give to others. This was Christian compassion where the people freely gave to their brothers and sisters who had needs.

How much can be done for the cause of Christ when the church learns to give? Our resources are not given to us merely for us to have more. God provides for us so that we can use that provision to make a difference in the world for his glory. Learning to give cheerfully is the responsibility and the blessing of every believer.

Fourth, a passionate church is a worshiping church. Verses 46 and 47 describe the church as a worshiping church. They had an attitude of worship that transcended mere religious formality. They were genuinely interested in praising God because he is worthy of praise.

True worship always has an impact on the world. The impact of their praise of God was "having favor with all the people." The world is looking for something—really, for Someone—who is worthy of praise. The church knows the only One who is worthy. We have the privilege of worshiping our Lord corporately in our worship services. And, we can worship the Lord day by day in our individual lives and gatherings. He is truly worthy of our worship. Therefore, a passionate church has passionate worship.

Food for Thought

The church is never stronger than when it is living with passion. The passion of your own Christian life will lead you to follow the example of the first church. It will be evidenced by your own passion for outreach, learning, giving, and worship. Which of these areas is the weakest in your life?

Faith in Action

Ask yourself these questions and then take action. Who can I share the gospel with today? What specific things am I doing to learn more and grow in my walk with God? Do I need to connect with a church and/or a small group? What specific ways can I become more generous with the resources God has provided me? Is worship an important of my daily life? Reading a devotional commentary like 30 Days to Acts is a great way to grow in your personal walk with God. Consider reading through it with another believer and challenging one another to continue growing.

Prayer

Ask God to help you to have greater passion for reaching the lost, learning the word, joyfully giving, and worshiping with all your heart. Ask the Lord to fill you with passion for the things of God. Commit to go beyond the motions of religion to a life of passion for the things that matter eternally.

What I Do Have

Acts 3:1-10

I have no silver and gold, but what I do have I give to you. In the name of Jesus Christ of Nazareth, rise up and walk!
Acts 3:6

It is hard to overestimate the difficulties in the life of the man in our Scripture verses today. Absolutely dependent upon others to carry him to his destinations, unable to provide income for food and necessities without begging, and a constant object of pity and even scorn; his life was hard. But, it was the only life he had known. Lame from birth, he had never known the joy of running across the soft grass or climbing a tree like the other boys. As for the temple, it was merely a convenient place to beg for handouts. He could never imagine actually entering to worship with the others, because he was banned from entering because of his infirmity. He was a lame beggar. He was destined to live on the fringes of society, hoping for the scraps that came from the kindness or the guilt of those around him.

Acts 3 tells the remarkable story of this man and his encounter with Peter and John. It seemed to be a day like any other. It was the ninth hour, about three in the afternoon, and Peter and John were headed to the temple to pray. People brought the crippled man this day, as they did every day, to the gate leading into the temple. There he lay

Our past does not have to dictate our future.

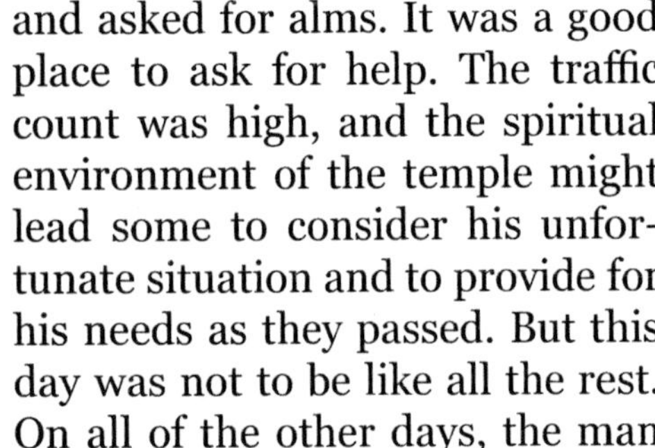

and asked for alms. It was a good place to ask for help. The traffic count was high, and the spiritual environment of the temple might lead some to consider his unfortunate situation and to provide for his needs as they passed. But this day was not to be like all the rest. On all of the other days, the man hoped to receive money. On this day, the man received far more.

Two lessons should be noted here. First, note that our future can be different than our past. God can make all things new. A miraculous healing touch allowed the man of this story to walk. Forgiveness and a fresh touch from God can lead our futures to be very different from our past. God can provide the victory over our past that we need so desperately. Our past does not have to dictate our future.

Second, God's plans are better than our plans. The man of the story asked for money. He would have considered it a great day had he received a large donation. But God's plan for him was far greater; God planned to give him fully functioning limbs and abilities he had never known. We may dream of gold, yet God tells us of streets lined with the stuff. We may plan for the moment, but God tells us of his plans for eternity. Better to follow God's plans for our lives than our own, because God's plans are far greater and better than ours.

Verse four tells us that Peter and John noticed this crippled man. The man thought they were going to give him money, so he fixed his gaze on them. How disappointed he must have been when Peter said, "I have no silver and gold." How shocked he must have been to hear him continue, "But what I do have I give to you. In the name of Jesus Christ of Nazareth, rise up and walk!" Peter didn't stop there. He reached down and did something no one had ever done to him before—he pulled him to his feet.

Suddenly, there was unexpected strength in those feet and ankles.

The Lord provided two things for this crippled man on that day—healing and opportunity. One provision made by the Lord was for healing. The man was able, for the first time in his life, to walk, run, and jump. For the first time he was no longer a cripple.

I suppose one reason this story is so meaningful to me is because my own grandfather was crippled. Due to an accident as a boy, one leg did not grow properly. This left my grandfather with a severe and debilitating limp for the rest of his life. My grandfather was never healed physically on this earth. My grandfather certainly discovered spiritual healing, however.

As a middle-aged man, my grandfather heard the message of the gospel. He placed his trust in Jesus who died and rose again, and he repented of his sins. He was saved from his sins by the power of the Savior, and he found new life in Christ. Though his leg remained weak, his soul found strength in the Lord Jesus. For the first time in his life he found salvation, forgiveness, and grace. He was healed in a far greater way than mere physical healing. Those who need the Lord's strength over sin's grip should still seek spiritual healing today.

A second provision made by the Lord was opportunity. Think of all of the opportunities that opened to this man in Acts 3. He could find employment instead of begging. He could travel, visit his friends, and dance. But one opportunity found expression in his life immediately; he began to worship. Think of the joy of that moment when this man walked into the temple for the first time and began to worship God both personally and corporately.

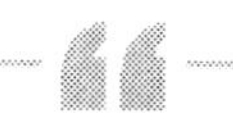

Recognize the joy, wonder, and privilege of worship.

While worship is always open to us no matter our physical condition, this man found new expression in worship. Verse eight

See the opportunity we have to worship the Lord who is powerful, eternal, and loving.

records him walking, leaping, and praising God. His thankfulness for God's work in his life led him to a physical and tangible expression. And, note the first place his new legs took him. This verse tells us "he entered the temple." This was the first time this formerly crippled man had ever been allowed inside the temple. Now he was able to walk in and worship the Lord who filled that temple.

Worship can be taken for granted by many believers. It can become nothing more than a habit or a formality. Some Christians see it as drudgery or merely a responsibility. How much better it is to recognize the joy, wonder, and privilege of worship. How much greater it is to see the opportunity we have to worship the Lord who is powerful, eternal, and loving. The man who was healed immediately turned to worship, expressing his love and thankfulness to God.

Verses nine and ten tell the result of the man's healing and subsequent worship. The people saw what had happened. A true miracle had taken place in the man physically, and this could not be denied. And, they noticed the spirit of thankfulness and worship that now filled him. The Bible tells us "they were filled with wonder and amazement." There was a groundswell of interest in matters of Jesus Christ. There was a renewed focus on genuine worship. And God would use this event as a catalyst for his work in Jerusalem, and ultimately, throughout the world.

The crippled man didn't get the money that he sought that day. Instead, he got something far better. And from that day on he would not go to the temple to beg for alms—he would go to the temple to give praise to the God who changes lives.

Food for Thought

God changes lives. He can change our broken past into a bright tomorrow. His plans are always better than our plans. When we discover and follow God's better plan for our lives it always leads to worship and that worship always leads to witness.

Faith in Action

Write down a specific time of God's healing in your life (physical or spiritual). Did you acknowledge it as God's miraculous touch? Stop to thank him now for his healing touch in your life. What are some specific ways that your worship of God can be a witness to others?

Prayer

Pray for God to give you appreciation for his power to heal physically, and even more importantly, spiritually. Ask him to give you greater enthusiasm for worshiping him fully. Ask him to show you how your worship can be a witness to others. Thank him for the many blessings he has provided to you—especially the gift of salvation.

Times of Refreshing

Acts 3:11-26

Repent therefore, and turn back, that your sins may be blotted out, that times of refreshing may come from the presence of the Lord.
Acts 3:18-19

If you have ever been really hot and tired, you know the joy of refreshment. Maybe after some yard work on a summer's day, or after a strenuous workout, you have enjoyed that moment when you get a cold drink and relax in a comfortable chair. How refreshing! Far greater than that is the spiritual refreshment we can find in the Lord Jesus Christ. God offers rest to the sin-wearied soul. The Lord provides the rejuvenating energy of his Holy Spirit. True refreshment is found in the Lord.

Peter saw the crowd that congregated at the portico of the temple. They were gathered in astonishment at the great miracle that had occurred. A grown man, lame from birth, had been healed in the name of Jesus. This man entered the temple praising God and leaping on newly strengthened legs. Peter saw the

True refreshment is found in the Lord.

We put Jesus on the cross by our own sins; our iniquity drove the nails into his hands and feet.

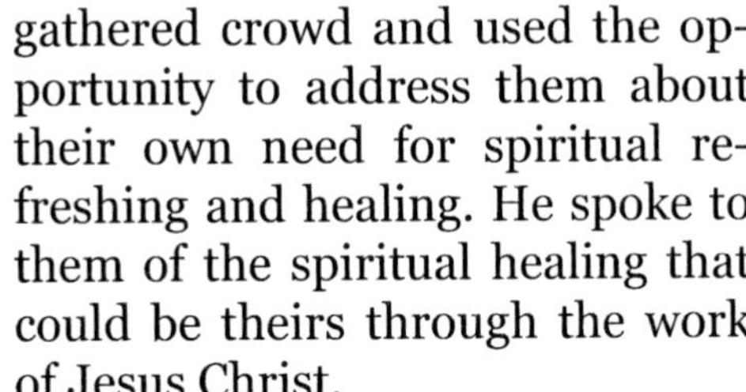

gathered crowd and used the opportunity to address them about their own need for spiritual refreshing and healing. He spoke to them of the spiritual healing that could be theirs through the work of Jesus Christ.

Perhaps those in Israel who listened to Peter preach had an advantage. Living in that dry and dusty land, they knew the refreshment that came when the cooling rains finally arrived. They understood the rejuvenation that occurred and the beauty and abundance that followed. When Peter spoke of their need for times of refreshing, the people who heard could easily imagine their need for the rejuvenating work of God's Spirit. They knew the cracked ground of their hearts and the parched soil of their souls.

Peter's sermon to the gathered crowd had three principles to teach. First, he told the people and us, that we have a need. This need is evidenced by our rejection of God's best. In verse 13, Peter told the listening group how God had sent Jesus to them. We are reminded that God's eternal plan was for Jesus to come into our world to meet our need. The great need of mankind is to destroy sin. Sin separates us from God. Sin robs us of our purpose and destroys God's plans for us. Ultimately, sin always leads to death and separation from God.

Our need is great. The Bible reminds us that "all have sinned and fall short of the glory of God (Rom 3:23)," and that "the wages of sin is death (Rom 6:23)." These verses speak to our incredible need. We are all sinners and the consequences of our sin are tragic, lasting, and eternal.

Not only have we rejected God's best for our lives, but also Peter reminded his hearers, and us, that we are responsible for Christ's death. In verse 14 he told his hearers that they "denied the Holy and Righteous One, and asked for a murderer." That is, they called for the release of Barabbas and demanded the crucifixion of Jesus. To emphasize the injustice of what happened, Peter declared in verse 15, "You killed the Author of life, whom God raised from the dead." These accusations were not designed to tickle ears but to convict hearts. Peter told his audience the hard truth.

Lest we consider the death of Jesus to be merely the result of the Jews and Romans choices long ago, we should consider that our own sins are the reason that Jesus died. He died willingly in our place and for our sins. When picturing the Roman soldiers driving the nails into the hands and feet of the Savior, we should look more closely. In doing so, we can see with our spiritual eyes that the faces of those soldiers are our own. We put Jesus on the cross by our own sins; our iniquity drove the nails into his hands and feet.

The second principle of Peter's message was that we have a remedy. From the beginning of the message Peter noted that Jesus was the one who met the needs of the lame man, and Jesus was the one who could meet their needs as well. Not only does the Lord point out our need, he has done something to meet that need. The power of Jesus to heal the lame man points to his ability to provide the remedy for our needs.

Verses 17-20 point out that Jesus not only has the power to heal physically, he has the power to heal spiritually. That is, his power is great enough to forgive the guilty. Sinners can be forgiven of their sins. The guilty can be forgiven of their guilt. Note the call to repentance found in verse 19: we are called to do our part—repent. The Lord does his part—he forgives and refreshes our souls. Our part is repentance; the Lord's part is forgiveness and restoration.

> *"Jesus has the power to heal spiritually."*

The third principle Peter told the crowd in his sermon was that we have a testimony. We have the testimony of the prophets. We are reminded of the words of the prophets in verses 21-25. All the

Our part is repentance; the Lord's part is forgiveness and restoration.

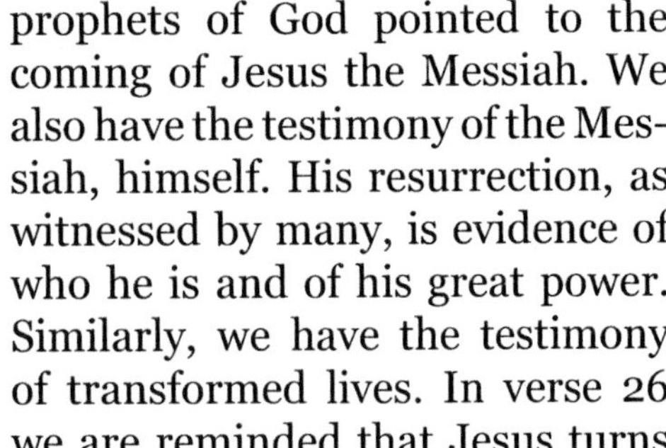

prophets of God pointed to the coming of Jesus the Messiah. We also have the testimony of the Messiah, himself. His resurrection, as witnessed by many, is evidence of who he is and of his great power. Similarly, we have the testimony of transformed lives. In verse 26 we are reminded that Jesus turns us from our wickedness. He transforms our souls and, in so doing, he transforms the very fabric and character of our lives.

The miracle of the healing of the man paralyzed from birth gave occasion to speak to an even greater miracle. The healing of a body lasts for a time, but Jesus offers the healing of our souls which lasts for eternity. We can discover this great truth for ourselves by repenting of our sins and trusting Jesus Christ as our Savior and Lord. And through this we discover the refreshing touch of God's forgiveness, grace, and power. We discover the refreshing joy God brings to our souls through his Son, Jesus Christ.

Food for Thought

God wants you to experience refreshment in your soul that comes through repenting of your sins and placing your faith in him. This miracle of salvation is even greater than physical healing as it makes a difference deep within and lasts for eternity. If you haven't yet experienced salvation, today could be the day you discover this joy in your own soul. Turn from your sins and trust the Lord Jesus who died and rose again. He can give you this new life and can heal your very soul. For more about how to do this, please read "Finding L.I.F.E. in Jesus" at the end of this book. If you have trusted Christ, ask the Lord to draw you closer to him and to his purposes for you.

Faith in Action

Despite the fact that God has forgiven our sin debt, we still battle temptation while we live in this world. And, at times we may even yield to that temptation. When we sin, we don't lose our salvation, but we do grieve God's heart. This is why we must practice confession for daily sin as part of our daily prayer life. Jesus describes this in his model prayer (Mt 6:13-15), and John gives us this word of instruction and encouragement: "If we confess our sins, he is faithful and just to forgive us our sins and to cleanse us from all unrighteousness (1 Jn 1:9)." Should you sin today, practice personal confession. We experience God's refreshment in our hearts as we walk in close fellowship with him!

Prayer

Thank God for the work of the Lord Jesus for you on the cross. Acknowledge that your sins put Jesus on the cross and thank him for the great love he has shown to you. Thank him for the refreshing touch he brings to your soul as you trust and follow him. Thank him for offering salvation full and free through the death and resurrection of Jesus Christ.

There is No Other Name

Acts 4:1-12

There is salvation in no one else, for there is no other name under heaven given among men by which we must be saved.
Acts 4:12

Our name represents who we are. When someone hears your name, they think of you and what they know of you. They remember your good and bad traits, your actions and attitudes, and the kind of person you are, or at least what they can see of who you are. Your name represents you.

The name of Jesus reminds us who he is. We remember the teachings in the Bible about him. We remember his entrance into humanity at Bethlehem, his death for humanity at the cross, and his provision for humanity in the resurrection. His name represents who he is.

The name Jesus means "Savior." He was given this name because he is the Savior of the world. In fact, our focal verse reminds us that he is the only one who can save us. Salvation is found in no one else. Jesus' very name reminds us of this truth.

Acts 4 begins with the arrest of Peter and John. They had been preaching the message of the gospel that Jesus

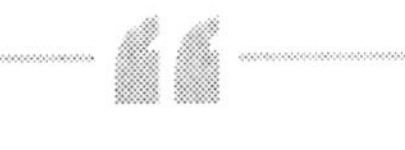

Salvation is found in no one else. Jesus' very name reminds us of this truth.

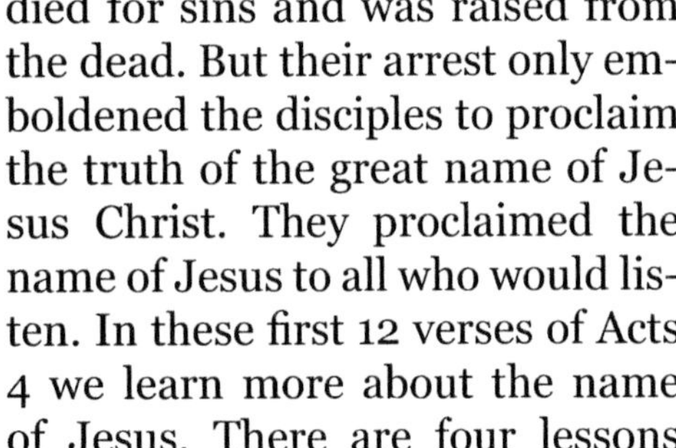

died for sins and was raised from the dead. But their arrest only emboldened the disciples to proclaim the truth of the great name of Jesus Christ. They proclaimed the name of Jesus to all who would listen. In these first 12 verses of Acts 4 we learn more about the name of Jesus. There are four lessons about the name of Jesus every believer should learn from this passage.

First, these verses teach us that the name of Jesus brings controversy. The name of Jesus was controversial in the early days of the church, and it is still controversial today. In the New Testament, Peter and John were arrested for proclaiming the truth of that great name. Many in our world today face great persecution because of the name of Jesus.

Our nation doesn't yet face the persecution that happens in some parts of the world, but there is growing opposition to the name of Jesus. It is considered controversial to pray in Jesus' name in the public arena. Soft, "non-sectarian prayers" are acceptable, but not prayer in the powerful name of our Savior. On college campuses it is becoming less acceptable all the time to mention the name of our Lord in a positive way. And stating the biblical claim that Jesus is the only way to salvation is considered narrow and bigoted. Will the day come soon when following Jesus will bring imprisonment in America? Will believers in this land face the same sort of persecution that was faced in the days of the early church? And, if it does, will you be faithful in the face of that persecution as were Peter and John?

The name of Jesus is controversial, but Peter and John were willing to face imprisonment, and even death for the sake of Jesus. Peter was powerfully changed by that name. Before the death of Jesus, he denied that he knew him three times. After the resurrection, he preached the name with boldness despite threats and imprisonment.

A second thing this passage teaches us is that the name of Jesus brings converts. Despite the controversy surrounding the message of the gospel, many believed. They saw the miraculous power of Jesus to heal the lame. They heard the miraculous message of Jesus to forgive sins. And, many of those who heard gave their lives to Jesus as their Savior and Lord.

Verse four tells us that the number of men who trusted Jesus for salvation came to about five thousand. Think of that—five thousand men trusted Christ as their Savior. The early church grew phenomenally, not because of elaborate programs or because of their great political power, but because of the power of the name of Jesus. They grew because of the power of Jesus to change lives and eternity. They grew because Jesus had changed their lives and used them to help others discover that same life-changing truth.

Nothing is more important to growing our churches than the name of Jesus. Great churches are not built on programs, though we are thankful for our programs. Great churches aren't built on beautiful music or powerful preaching, although those things are good. Great churches are built on the great name of Jesus. He is the one who builds and sustains the church, and he deserves all the praise and glory.

Third, these verses tell us that the name of Jesus brings clarity. We are told in verse five through seven that Peter and John were brought before the religious authorities,. The high priest and others from his family were there, along with the Sadducees and other leaders. They asked a simple question. "By what power or by what name did you do this?"

Using this opportunity, Peter spoke to them about the work of Jesus. Note that verse eight tells us that Peter was filled with the Holy Spirit. These weren't merely the words of Peter. God was speak-

> *The early church grew, not because of elaborate programs or great political power, but because of the power of the name of Jesus.*

He is either the only means of our salvation or Peter's declaration was a lie.

ing the truth to the people through Peter. Peter told the authorities in clear terms that the miraculous healing of the lame man was done by the name of Jesus Christ of Nazareth. He wanted them to clearly understand the power of Jesus to do this miracle. And, he told the gathered authorities that this was the same Jesus whom they had crucified. But that despite the crucifixion, Jesus was alive. In verse ten he tells his hearers that Jesus was the one who died and whom "God raised from the dead."

With a clear witness and great courage, Peter told his captors of their own sinful action in crucifying Jesus and of the Father's great power in raising him from the dead. He described Jesus as the stone they had rejected and which God had made the chief cornerstone of faith. He wanted there to be no ambiguity. Jesus was not just another prophet or a good teacher. Peter declared that he was the Savior of the world.

A final thing this passage teaches us is that the name of Jesus brings choices. Verse 12 is a powerful affirmation. Jesus is declared to be the only means of salvation. He is not described as one way to heaven, or as the best way to heaven. He is declared to be the only way to heaven and the only means by which we can be saved from the penalty of sin. Men and women hearing these words are left with a choice. Do we believe this about Jesus or do we not? Do we acknowledge him as our Savior or do we not? Do we declare with the apostles his authority over sin, death, and hell or do we not?

We are not left with the option of thinking Jesus was just a good man or a fine teacher. He is either the only means of our salvation or Peter's declaration was a lie. As for me, I will join Peter in this great declaration of faith. "There is salvation in no one else, for there is no other name under heaven given among men by which we must be saved." Won't you join me?

Food for Thought

There is great power in the name of Jesus. His name reminds us of the truth that he is the Savior of the world and the only means by which we can be forgiven of sin and obtain eternal life. We are reminded that through his great name we can see our lives, and the lives of others, transformed by the power of the gospel. Though controversial to many, the name of Jesus is the only one that can provide hope, meaning, and purpose.

Faith in Action

The boldness of Peter before his captors reminds us of the surpassing value of Jesus. His belief in the powerful name of Jesus gave him the courage to proclaim the only truth that changes lives. Actions always reveal what we truly believe. What do you do when faced with an opportunity to share Jesus? Are you bold or do you shrink back? Do you really believe that Jesus is the only way for those you love to find hope, meaning and purpose in life? Take time to evaluate your actions and your witness. What do they reveal about your own belief in the name of Jesus? How can you be more intentional about sharing your faith in Jesus?

Prayer

Ask God to give you boldness like Peter had to witness of the truth of Jesus even in the face of adversity. Thank the Lord for the forgiveness of sins he gives through Jesus' death and resurrection, and ask the Lord to help you to live with confidence in his great truth and power.

We Can't Stop

Acts 4:13-22

They recognized that they had been with Jesus.
Acts 4:13

God surprises us with the people he chooses to use in his work—carpenters, fishermen, you, me. What is he thinking? How can he use such simple people; people who have messed up and fallen short and don't have their acts together? How can he use people who lack supernatural abilities and don't fit the mold?

When God called me to vocational ministry, it was such a surprise. Sure, I had committed my life to God and told him I wanted to do whatever he wanted me to do. But, become a preacher? I was too sensitive. I was too shy. In fact, I was so scared of public speaking that I waited until my very last semester of college to take the required class in that subject. I don't know if you know this, but pastors have to do a lot of public speaking!

But God knew what he was doing. He knew that he was able to use me in spite of my obvious weaknesses. In fact, God wanted to use my weakness as a means of teaching me to trust him more. It's true for you too. The more we trust God, the stronger we become.

The rulers, elders, and scribes who gathered together to examine Peter and John in Acts 4 did not expect men like this to be causing such a theological stir. In fact, they were astonished by these men. Peter and John were uneducated, common men. But their boldness was remarkable

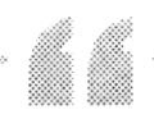

Without an anchor in the truth we can be pushed and pulled by every new wind that blows through our culture.

and impossible to ignore. And, they recognized that these men had been with Jesus.

These verses delineate clearly for us the difference between religion-based deadness and relationship-based boldness. The accusers were religious and dead. They had great educations and important titles, but they didn't know God. The accused had none of the trappings of success. They had no formal education to speak of, but they did have one very important thing—they had a relationship with the Lord Jesus that led to spiritual boldness, power, and effectiveness. Let's note the differing characteristics between religion-based deadness and relationship-based boldness.

First, religion-based deadness ignores life-changing faith. Verse 14 says, "But seeing the man who was healed standing beside them, they had nothing to say in opposition." They no more had an answer to the miracle of God's healing than does the modern skeptic to the evidence of God's greatness revealed in creation. Their answer was to ignore the truth and move on.

Second, religion-based deadness stifles the spread of the gospel message. Though they could not deny the miracle that had taken place, they did not want the foundational truth of this miracle to spread. After all, the spread of faith in Jesus could be bad for the business of religion. Better to stamp out this enthusiasm. Better to keep this truth from spreading. And so, they called Peter and John before them and gave them a demand—no more speaking or teaching in the name of Jesus.

In modern times, religion can stifle the spread of the gospel in several ways. Some change the meaning of the gospel. The gospel may be changed to mean "be good" or "go to church." Some change the work of the gospel. Mission trips become sight-seeing or merely meeting the physical needs of others without pointing them to Jesus who meets their deeper, spiritual needs. Or, some stifle the gospel through persecution. Christians in some parts of the world face persecution, and often it comes at the hands of religious leaders.

Third, religion-based deadness succumbs to popular opinion. Verse 21 tells us that they threatened Peter and John but could do no more. Popular opinion was behind these men for the moment, and the religious leaders were more concerned with pleasing the people and keeping their power than in pursuing the truth. Without an anchor in the truth we can be pushed and pulled by every new wind that blows through our culture.

In contrast, this text reveals three notable aspects of relationship-based boldness. First, relationship-based boldness starts with knowing Jesus. Note the key characteristic of these Peter and John—they had been with Jesus. They knew him, they followed him, and they were used by him to make an impact in the world. They were uneducated and untrained, but their relationship with the Lord led to a bold faith and power that astonished the world.

Second, relationship-based boldness submits to God's best. Verse 19 records the response of Peter and John to the religious leaders' demand that they no longer speak in the name of Jesus. In effect, they asked a question of them. "Do you think it's better for us to obey you or to obey God?" Should we follow your wishes or the heart of the Lord? To whom should we submit? Clearly they believed submitting to God superior to submitting to men.

Third, relationship-based boldness spills over in witness. Verse 20 highlights the attitude of these followers of Jesus. "We cannot but speak of what we have seen and heard." This was not just a religion that one adheres to out of fear, obligation, or tradition. This was a relationship that had so transformed their lives that they could not help but tell others. It had to be shared.

The Lord wants more than mere religious ritual from us. He wants a relationship that transforms us and empowers us.

Acts 4:13-22

The Lord wants more than mere religious ritual from us. He wants a relationship that transforms us and empowers us. That relationship leads to our bold declaration of faith to our world. That relationship empowers us to be used by God despite our lack of education, training, ability, or wealth. God in us is the key to spiritual power. Education is good. Training is helpful. But nothing can replace spending time in the presence of Jesus. Nothing can replace our relationship with him.

Spend time with Jesus today. Spend time with him in his word and let him instruct your life. Spend time with him in prayer and let him hear your heart. Nothing can replace time spent with Jesus. Let your life be about more than religion, power, fame, or wealth. Spend time with him and you will discover the power for life that he wants you to enjoy. You will discover the power for witness that he wants you to unleash, and others will recognize that you have been with Jesus.

Food for Thought

God wants more than just religious activity from you. He wants a personal relationship with you that begins with salvation and leads to a deepening fellowship with him. Nothing can replace time spent with the Lord. This 30 Days to Acts experience can be the start or continuation of a regular devotional life. Spending time each day reading the Bible will help you to gain understanding and insight into God's plan for your life. It will help you to know the Lord more intimately and serve him more effectively. Spending time each day in prayer will help you to develop a closeness and connection with God. As you praise him and share your needs with him, you will deepen your fellowship with the Lord.

Faith in Action

Ask yourself, "Can those around me tell that I have been with Jesus? Is there anything different about me?" Commit to the spiritual discipline of a regular devotional time with the Lord. Like consistent exercise develops the physical body, regular devotions will develop you spiritually. It will make a difference in your life. Commit to spending quality time in prayer and Bible reading at least 5 days each week. If you don't already do this, start today!

Prayer

Ask the Lord to help you to grow closer in your relationship with him. Call on him to help your relationship with him become so evident to others that they can see that you know him as your Savior and your Lord. Ask the Lord to help your love for him grow so much that it can't help but overflow in your words and witness.

When You Lie to God

Acts 5:1-11

And great fear came upon the whole church and upon all who heard of these things.
Acts 5:11

The fear of the Lord. It sounds so antiquated to our ears. It is an old-fashioned concept that sounds to modern believers like stories told to them by their grandparents about steam engines or the days before computers. Surely it doesn't apply today, does it?

The fear of the Lord is a common Bible theme and much needed today. But it is often misunderstood. It is not that we fear an unjust God who is looking for an opportunity to harm us. It is that we recognize the holiness and majesty of God, and we recognize his righteous judgment. We acknowledge that he rightly judges our sins and our shortcomings. But this fear of God's judgment is connected to our relationship with him as our loving Lord. God is both holy and loving.

When I was young, I had a healthy fear of the consequences that came with disobedience to my parents. I knew my parents loved me, and I knew they wanted the best for me. They weren't looking for opportunities to harm me. But, I also knew they were committed to disciplining

God is both holy and loving.

me when I did wrong. And, deep inside, I knew that discipline was connected to their love for me. I feared the consequences that came from my parents when I chose the wrong path. I had a healthy respect for them and for their responsibility to discipline me.

If the church accepts the love of God without accepting the holiness of God, they will not fear God and his discipline. If the church sees only the blessings of faith without the responsibilities of faith, they will not fear God and his righteous judgment. Rightly understood, the fear of God is a healthy part of the life of the Christian and the church. The early church got a clear lesson on the consequences of disobedience to the Lord through the powerful and tragic story found in the first verses of Acts 5.

The story of Ananias and Sapphira was preceded by a time of great expansion and generosity. The early church exploded in growth, but was also exceptionally generous. People gave generously so that anyone who had a need found that need met. Barnabas even sold a field and brought the money to the apostles so that needs in the church could be fulfilled. That kind of love, generosity, and concern for others was common in the early church.

We can imagine that this kind of generosity was greatly praised by the people in the church. Perhaps there was a buzz through the congregation as people noted the amazing example of Barnabas in giving this money from the sale of his property. Ananias and Sapphira could not have helped but notice the attention paid to Barnabas. Perhaps there was some jealousy over his popularity in the church. So they hatched a plan.

Ananias, with Sapphira's knowledge, sold a piece of property and brought part of the profit to the apostles. The difference between what they did and what Barnabas did was that they presented a partial amount as if it were the full amount. In other words, they plotted to lie and deceive. They may have been able to fool the church, but they couldn't fool God—they died at the church they tried to deceive. Fear gripped the whole church as they realized the serious nature and consequence of sin. The story of Ananias and Sapphira teaches us, just as it did the early church, some lessons on what is important. Four lessons in particular should be noted.

First, this story teaches us about the importance of honesty. Peter rebuked Ananias for lying. He noted that Ananias was not under compulsion to sell the property or to give the full amount if he did sell it. But, the dishonesty and deception of pretending to give the full amount was a serious sin. In fact, Peter noted in verse four that Ananias had not lied to the church; he had lied to God.

Peter noted the source of dishonesty in verse three. He said to Ananias, "Why has Satan filled your heart to lie to the Holy Spirit?" Jesus said of Satan in John 8:44, "When he lies, he speaks out of his own character, for he is a liar and the father of lies." Satan is the source of dishonesty, and when we lie we follow his example. The Lord is the source of honesty. He tells the truth and calls us to live out the truth. Honesty is important because it reflects the very nature and character of God.

Second, this story teaches us the importance of integrity. Someone has said that integrity is who you are when no one is looking. Ananias and Sapphira apparently wanted the same praise that had been given to Barnabas. But, they were not willing to live by the same standard of integrity that Barnabas displayed. They wanted the praise of men and the recognition of others, but they were unwilling to live the transparent life of integrity.

Honesty is important because it reflects the very nature and character of God.

God is concerned about who you are, not just how others perceive you. You might be able to fool others, but you can never fool God. The life of integrity is about

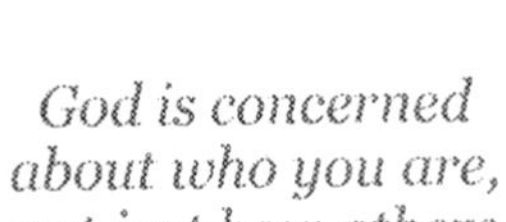

God is concerned about who you are, not just how others perceive you.

living by the standards of God's word both in public and in private. It is about obeying the Lord when it is noticed and when it is not. It is about who you are, not just what you say.

Third, the story of Ananias and Sapphira teaches us the importance of holiness. God takes holiness seriously. Over and over the Bible calls us to live holy lives. The death of this husband and wife reminded the early church how important that call really is. The early church and the church of today are given a vivid reminder that holiness always matters to the Lord because God is a holy God. The Lord wants his people to live out that standard of holiness. God wants us to reflect his character. This story is a clear indication of that truth.

Let me ask you a question. Does your life reflect God's holiness? Is there some action or attitude in your life that is less than holy? Is God convicting you of changes that need to be made in your life? Wise is the one who will heed that conviction and take holiness as seriously as the Lord takes it.

Fourth, this story teaches us the importance of our witness. The death of Ananias and Sapphira reminds us of the importance of our personal witness. The Lord takes hypocrisy very seriously. The early church was at a fragile point in development, and God sent a clear reminder of the need to avoid deceit and hypocrisy. What you do is a critical part of your witness. We don't just call Jesus our Lord; that lordship should be reflected in the things that we do and in the way that we live.

Perhaps someone is watching your life right now. "Do those Christians really mean what they say? Is this faith really genuine?" God uses our lives as witnesses of sin and righteousness, love and judgment. The quality of our lives is a witness to a seeking world.

The early church learned a critical lesson. God takes sin seriously. In salvation, the ultimate penalty for our sin is paid. But the call to holy living remains. We are to follow the model of our Savior who lived a holy life. We are to be holy because God is holy.

Food for Thought

God calls the church to live holy lives. Our honesty and integrity make a lasting impact upon our witness. As a result, God takes these issues seriously. Believers need to recognize that God is both loving and holy. We should have great respect for his just judgment and fear of the consequences of sin. Out of our love for him, and his love for us, we should seek to live our lives in a way that is consistent with his holy nature.

Faith in Action

Identify any attitudes or actions in your heart and life that need to be changed or corrected. Acknowledge to yourself and to God the seriousness of those sinful areas in your life. Where God shows you sinfulness in your life, repent and ask for his forgiveness and cleansing. Commit yourself to a life of honesty and integrity so that your witness for him shines through both your words and your deeds.

Prayer

Ask the Lord to make you a clean vessel that he can use to make an impact in the world for his glory. Ask him to bring conviction to your life where you have strayed and to use your life as you follow him and live by integrity. Praise him for his holiness and ask him to help you to live a holy life.

Obeying God or Man?

Acts 5:17-32

We must obey God rather than men.
Acts 5:29

Around the world, many face persecution for their faith in the Lord Jesus. We often hear news of Christians who are imprisoned, beaten, and even killed for their faith. In some parts of the world, persecution of Christians seems commonplace. This persecution is nothing new, of course. The early church knew a great deal about persecution. Acts 5 tells us that even the apostles were imprisoned for their faith. The religious leaders threw them into jail hoping to dampen their enthusiasm and slow down the explosive growth of the early church.

God, however, had different plans than the religious leaders. They threw the apostles in jail; the Lord miraculously set them free. In the middle of the night an angel of the Lord opened the prison doors and brought the disciples out. It must have seemed like a dream to those weary men in those squalid cells trying to sleep. But this was no dream. An angel of the Lord appeared to them, opened the prison doors and set them free.

Then, the angel told them to do something surprising. "Go" he commanded in verse 20, "and stand in the

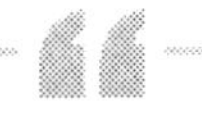

Men who have died to self in order to live for Christ are hard to intimidate.

temple and speak to the people all the words of this Life." Hmmm... wasn't that the sort of thing that got them thrown into prison to begin with? But the message came from the Lord and the apostles were in the habit of obeying God's commands.

What do you think you would have done in that situation? Argue? Run? Stop your ears with your fingers and loudly hum? The immediate response of the apostles was obedience. At daybreak they were found in the temple teaching the message of the gospel.

The high priest and the other religious leaders were unaware of the work of the midnight angel. So they went about their business of calling a council of the senate and sending word to the prison to bring over the prisoners for interrogation. Only the prisoners weren't there. The prison authorities reported some confounding news. It seemed the prison was securely locked and the guards were at their posts, but the prisoners were nowhere to be found.

Just as this perplexing news was sinking in, more news arrived. Someone burst into the room to announce that the very men they were seeking were standing in the temple and teaching everyone who would listen. What a twist of events! So, the religious leaders sent the officers to bring the apostles to stand before the council. Fearing the people, they didn't do this by force, but instead had the men brought to them hoping to intimidate them. But men who have died to self in order to live for Christ are hard to intimidate.

As the apostles stood before the council, the high priest reminded them, "We strictly charged you not to teach in this name (v. 28)." The message had been clear, but the disciples had disobeyed these religious authorities and their demands. Instead, the apostles had obeyed an even greater authority. They had committed to obey God rather than men.

When we obey God rather than men, at least three things happen. First, our loyalty is clear. Peter spoke for the rest of the apostles and declared their loyalty to God's plans and purposes rather than man's. He said, "We must obey God rather than men." Notice the word "must." This was not an option for these believers—or any serious believer. In salvation we declare that Jesus is Lord, and our faith demands that we obey him as Lord. And, when the question becomes whether we will obey men or obey God, our loyalty is put to the test. With the apostles we can declare our loyalty to God through our obedience to his leadership and direction. Our supreme loyalty is to our sovereign Lord.

A second result of obeying God rather than men is that our message is clear. In verses 30 and 31, Peter and the apostles used the occasion (as they used most occasions) to proclaim the message of the gospel. Peter reminded the gathered dignitaries that they killed Jesus by hanging him on a cross. But he also reminded them that the God of their fathers had raised Jesus from the dead and exalted him as leader and Savior. And, that this truth should be met with repentance that leads to forgiveness of sins.

Peter's proclamation of the gospel was clear and concise. He spoke of a cross and a resurrection. He spoke of repentance and forgiveness. At its heart, the gospel message is simple. But too often we complicate the message. The apostles cut to the chase. They were going to obey God rather than men because of the truth of this simple gospel message. Their loyalties were clear and their message was clear.

A third result of obeying God rather than men is that our witness is clear. Peter and the apostles proclaimed themselves to be witnesses of the events of which they spoke. They were there when

"With the apostles we can declare our loyalty to God through our obedience to his leadership and direction."

Jesus hung on a cross for the sins of the world. They were there when the tomb was found empty and the risen Jesus appeared to them on multiple occasions. They served as witnesses of the truth. They even proclaimed that witness all the way to the end, as most of them would become martyrs for their beliefs. No one could doubt the clarity of their gospel witness.

Peter spoke of another witness to the truth of this simple gospel message. The Holy Spirit, given to those who obey God, was a witness to the truth. He still is today. He convicts and convinces us of the truth. Before I repented of my own sins and placed my faith in Christ long years ago, I remember the clear witness of the Holy Spirit in my life. He convicted me of my sins and my need for Christ. His clear and gentle witness in my spirit drew me to the moment of repentance and salvation. I am grateful for the clear witness of family, church members, and preachers, and for the clear witness of God's Spirit to the truth of this life-changing message.

How about you? Will you join the apostles in declaring your obedience to the Lord rather than following the way of the world? Perhaps today you would boldly proclaim, "I must obey God rather than men."

Food for Thought

The world is always telling us to follow and conform. But God has a far better way. God wants us to follow his better plan and live in obedience to him rather than men. The deeper our faith becomes, the more we will join the apostles in declaring that we "must" obey the Lord instead of the world. Our loyalty is to God and his direction for our lives, so we must join him in becoming witnesses of the clear message of the gospel.

Faith in Action

Identify a specific way that the world or people of the world encourage you to follow and conform. The ability to identify the world's demands will help you to resist them. Like the apostles, we can recognize the clear choice before us of living in obedience to either the world or to the Lord. And, like the apostles, we can make our loyalties clear. We are going to obey the Lord and his plans rather than obeying the world.

Prayer

Ask the Lord to strengthen your loyalties so that they will be clear. Declare your obedience to God rather than to man. Commit to obeying him rather than following the world's standards. And ask the Lord to use this commitment to help you be a faithful witness to clearly present the message of truth to the world desperately in need of that truth.

Called to Serve

Acts 6:1-7

Therefore, brothers, pick out from among you seven men of good repute, full of wisdom, whom we will appoint to this duty.
Acts 6:3

Acts 5 ends with the early church continuing to thrive. Acts 6 begins with complaints. Complaints have always been a part of church life because churches are made up of people who like to complain. Lest we idolize the people of the early church, we should remind ourselves that they were still people, and people have problems.

I've often joked that churches would be great if it weren't for the people. But, of course, churches are made up of people. And people have needs, issues, hurts, and problems. It is what makes church life messy and what makes the church so necessary. Let's note some lessons we learn from the early church and how they dealt with what could have been a disastrous moment in their infancy.

The first lesson we should note is this obvious truth: every church faces challenges. Note that I said "every" church. There are no perfect churches; there are no perfect pastors; there are no perfect church members. Therefore, every church faces challenges.

The problem faced by the church in Acts 6 concerned widows. Apparently, the Hellenistic widows were being neglected in their needs. The church was providing

Problems in a church can arise because a church is thriving.

for the needs of their most vulnerable members, but the widows from non-Jewish backgrounds were not receiving the same treatment as the Hebrew widows. As you might imagine, people began to complain.

Note that this complaint arose "in these days when the disciples were increasing in number (v. 1)." Even though the early church was thriving there were still problems. The same is true in the church today. Problems in a church can arise because a church is thriving. Churches will experience either problems from growth or problems from decline. I would rather have growth problems.

First Baptist Church of O'Fallon, Illinois, where I pastor, has grown a lot over the years. And that growth has caused some problems. One of those growth problems is finding space. For seven years I preached the weekend message at four different services because of our space problems. We have built many different buildings and had to raise money to pay for them each time. However, these are better problems than the problems that come with decline.

The danger of the problem faced by the early church was the real possibility of fractured unity. God wants our churches to live in unity. We have the same Lord, the same faith, and the same mission. But, problems can present challenges to that unity. The enemy wants to divide and conquer us. But God calls us to unity. The early church faced a real danger to that unity, so the church leaders took steps to maintain a unified spirit.

A second lesson we can learn from this passage is that effective churches make wise choices. At this critical juncture in the history of the church the apostles, under the leadership of the Holy Spirit, chose seven men who would serve the widows and the church. These seven were the first deacons.

The apostles' wise choice came out of their priorities. They had a responsibility to preach, and they did not want that to be sidelined by anything. The seven deacons were chosen so that the apostles could devote themselves "to prayer and to the ministry of the word (v. 4)."

The deacons at the church where I serve as pastor serve our church in such a fashion that I am able to focus on God's priorities for me. I cannot meet the needs of every widow in our congregation, but our deacons can. I cannot meet every need in our church, so our deacons help shoulder the load. I am able to give my energy to the priorities God has given me—preaching and prayer—because of the service of these godly men.

The apostles' wise choice came out of their understanding of roles and gifts. Not all are called to preach, but all are called to some area of service and responsibility. These men had a part to play in the work of God's church, even as every Christian has a part to play in the work of God's kingdom. God has a role for you to fill in the work of his church and his kingdom.

The apostles' wise choice came out of their understanding of godly leadership. They called on the church to choose seven men "full of the Holy Spirit and of wisdom (v. 3)." The ministry and service these men provided in the early church came out of their deep commitment to the Lord. They were godly men, not just willing men. The seriousness with which they undertook this task is demonstrated in verse six. The apostles "prayed and laid their hands on them." The seven were set apart in ordination for the important task given them by God. And, they were reminded of their dependence upon the Lord for the outcome.

What was the result of these decisions by the early church leaders? Was the church destined to derail in her infancy? What is the rest of the story? A third lesson we learn from this passage is that God

Every Christian has a part to play in the work of God's kingdom.

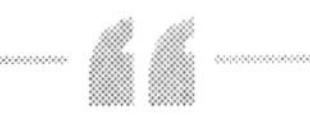

Instead of focusing on their problems, the church focused on the mission.

blesses faithfulness to His word. The unifying service of these seven godly deacons had a tremendous influence on the future of the church. Instead of floundering under controversy, the church expanded. Instead of focusing on their problems, the church focused on the mission.

Verse seven tells us, "The word of God continued to increase." That is, the message of God's word continued to be proclaimed clearly and boldly. The verse continues with the words, "And the number of the disciples multiplied greatly." That is, the mission of the church stayed sharp. They continued to reach people with the saving message of the gospel. And, the verse continues, "A great many of the priests became obedient to the faith." That is, the miraculous power of the gospel was fully displayed.

Far from being derailed, the early church moved forward like a locomotive. Such is the power of service. Such is the benefit of godly servants. Such is the power of the Holy Spirit working through the life of the church of our living Savior.

Food for Thought

Controversy is nothing new in the life of the church. But wise and godly leadership can bring unity and connection to the church, enabling her to perform her mission. Deacons who are filled with the Holy Spirit and wisdom can be a great blessing to the unity and mission of the church by their service. Any godly service is a great blessing to the work of God's church and God's kingdom.

Faith in Action

Service in God's church and God's kingdom is not just for deacons. All have a part to play in his kingdom. God calls all of his children to godliness. And godliness leads to service. Where are you serving? If you don't have a place of service, talk to your church leaders about where you can serve. Also, evaluate whether you are helping your leaders to promote unity in your church.

Prayer

Ask the Lord to guard the unity of your church fellowship and to bless the mission of your church fellowship. Pray for your church leaders by name. Pray for the ministry of your deacons or other leadership as they serve the needs of those in your church family. Pray that all the members of your church will strengthen the unity and the mission of your church by serving. And pray that the word of God will continue to increase through the ministry of your local church.

The Sermon that Wins

Acts 7:51-60

Lord, do not hold this sin against them.
Acts 7:60

I have a great interest in sermons. Not everyone can say that, but having been a pastor for almost three decades, and having taught preaching classes as an adjunct professor, you can understand my interest in the subject. That's why I love Stephen's sermon as it's recorded in Acts 7. I like to call it "The Sermon that Wins," and such it is, just not as you may anticipate, however.

Stephen, you will recall, was a deacon—one of the original seven. While he was not called to be an apostle, God called him, as he calls all Christians, to be a faithful witness. So, Stephen taught and preached the truth of the gospel whenever he got the opportunity. God used him in powerful ways, and many people came to Christ as a result of his godly life and faithful proclamation of the truth. As a result of his successful ministry, Stephen was called before the religious authorities to give an account of his actions. Stephen used the occasion to preach, and what a sermon it was. Stephen's winning sermon teaches us three things about every winning sermon.

> *Stephen was more concerned about pleasing God by telling the truth than pleasing people by softening that truth.*

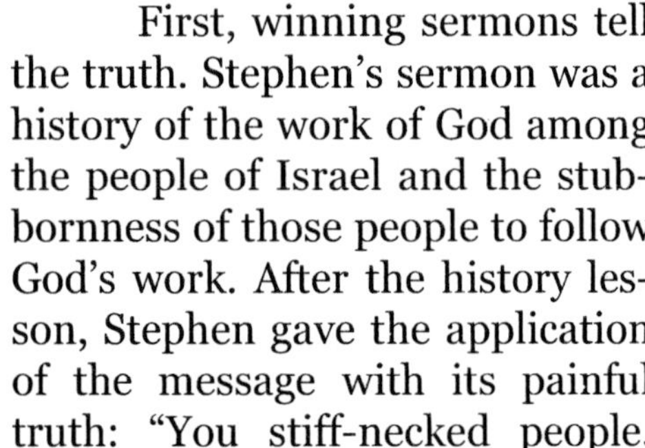

First, winning sermons tell the truth. Stephen's sermon was a history of the work of God among the people of Israel and the stubbornness of those people to follow God's work. After the history lesson, Stephen gave the application of the message with its painful truth: "You stiff-necked people, uncircumcised in heart and ears, you always resist the Holy Spirit (v. 51)." Did Stephen not go through the seminar on "How to Win Friends and Influence People?" What was he thinking? Didn't he know you have to go soft on folks?

The truth is, the truth can hurt. It can be painful to be told that you are sinning against God and his purposes. But the truth is the truth whether we like it or not. Stephen was more concerned about pleasing God by telling the truth than he was about pleasing people by softening that truth. Winning preaching always begins with telling God's truth. We don't, after all, preach our own words, we are preaching God's word. It isn't about what people want but about what they need.

Stephen even went so far as to tell the leaders that they had "betrayed and murdered" the Lord Jesus. The truth of the gospel is that our sins put Jesus on the cross. I am responsible for his death because he died for my sins.

The truth hurts, but the truth also heals. When we understand and apply the truth of God's word we can find the healing that comes through dealing with the pain of that truth. God calls us to the pain of confession so that we will find the forgiveness that follows repentance.

A second lesson we learn from Stephen's message is that winning sermons reach eternity. Winning sermons lead us to eternal matters rather than just making us feel better for the moment. They call us to the great rather than just the good. Stephen's message was concerned with heaven and hell and the everlasting issues of life.

Note the words "ground… gazed… glory" found in verses 54 and 55. They point us to the eternal nature of the sermon subject. We are told that the leaders "ground their teeth at him" upon hearing that they were responsible for the death of God's Son. Rather than dealing with the issue of sin and judgment, heaven and hell, they focused on their immediate anger at the message. They ground their teeth as a prelude to stoning the preacher to death. Preachers and Bible teachers don't be surprised if your audience doesn't respond to a message of truth as you had hoped.

Stephen, on the other hand, gazed into heaven. There he saw the glory of God and Jesus at the right hand of God the Father. His focus was already beyond this world to the real world, the eternal world that God had in store for him.

Once in a while, it serves the teacher, the deacon, the preacher, and any Christian, to stop for a moment and contemplate eternity. This world lasts for a few moments by comparison. One day, we will experience the never-ending land God has in store for us. We must never forget the reality of eternity. We must teach, preach, and live with eternity in mind. If you could gaze into heaven and be reminded of the glory of God, the reality of heaven, and the importance of Jesus, your life would count in ways that it would not otherwise.

The third lesson we are taught by Stephen's sermon is that winning sermons finish well. Any preacher will tell you that a strong conclusion really matters in a message. Of course, most listeners are just glad to get to the conclusion, period. Let's consider the conclusion of this amazing sermon.

Stephen's sermon conclusion was focused. Note that he preached his sermon conclusion while being stoned to death. That alone drew his focus to what really mattered. Stephen recognized his imminent death and focused on

Winning sermons lead us to eternal matters rather than just making us feel better for the moment.

Grudges and retribution tend to fade when we focus on all of the forgiveness that God has poured out on us.

his Savior, crying out "Lord Jesus, receive my spirit."

Stephen's sermon conclusion was forgiving. Amazingly, Stephen asked the Lord not to hold this sin against them (v. 60). Having been forgiven of his sins by the Lord Jesus, he desired the same forgiveness for others. Grudges and retribution tend to fade when we focus on all of the forgiveness that God has poured out on us.

Stephen's sermon conclusion was forever. This was his final message, his final lesson, and his final conclusion. The Bible says, "He fell asleep," which is to say that his life ended. But, in a way, the sermon conclusion never ended, for there was power to the witness of this winning sermon and its conclusion.

Acts 8 gives us a tantalizing piece of evidence that this sermon would continue to win. A man named Saul was there on the day that Stephen died. He listened to the sermon, he ground his teeth with the others, and he consented to the death of this godly preacher. But God would change his life and his forever, and he would soon preach the same kind of powerful sermons as Stephen. Now that is a sermon that wins!

Food for Thought

Stephen preached the truth of God. While it led to many coming to Christ in some cases, it led also to his murder—recorded in Acts 7. But whether well received or rejected, it was a winning sermon because it proclaimed God's truth under the leadership of the Holy Spirit.

Faith in Action

When you are confronted with a painful truth from God's word, how do you respond? Do you get defensive and try to rationalize your actions or attitudes? Do you get angry, deny your sinful actions, and even get mad at the preacher or teacher? Instead, ask God to reveal truth to you (Ps 139:23-24). As he reveals what is in your heart, confess and seek his forgiveness. He will forgive and help you walk in obedience to his word.

Prayer

Ask the Lord to make you a bold and truthful witness of his truth. Pray for the preachers, teachers, and others whom God puts in your life, that they would faithfully teach you the truth of God's word. Pray that your heart would always be receptive to God's truth.

The Gospel Comes to Africa

Acts 8:26-40

See, here is water! What prevents me from being baptized?
Acts 8:37

I am writing this chapter from Africa, where my daughter and her family serve as career missionaries with the International Mission Board of the Southern Baptist Convention. This is my fourth time on this vast continent, and I find myself amazed each time. The continent is massive, diverse, and fascinating.

One thing about the people of Africa that is exactly the same as people of every continent—they need the Lord. While there are vast numbers in Africa who do not have easy access to the gospel, or in some cases to the Bible written in their own language, there are thriving communities of faith in this land as well. Our devotional for today reminds us of how the message of salvation came to the land where some of my grandchildren are spending their childhoods.

The story involves another deacon named Philip and an Ethiopian court official. There are five principles this story teaches us about God's provision for our spiritual needs and ministries.

Ask the Lord to provide opportunities for you. The key is to be willing.

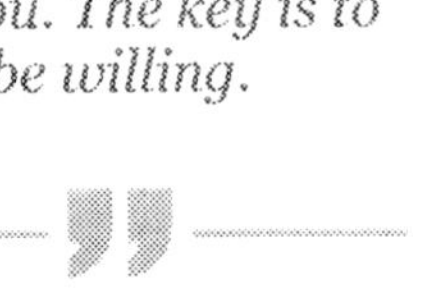

First, note that God provides opportunities for ministry. Following the martyrdom of Stephen, the church experienced persecution and scattered. Philip ended up in Samaria and began to proclaim the gospel. The crowds listened and responded, and many began to follow Christ.

In the midst of this great spiritual harvest, an angel came to Philip and told him to do something unusual. The angel told him to leave. Who leaves when things are going so great? And, not only did the angel tell him to leave, he told him to go to the desert road that led from Jerusalem to Gaza. It's one thing to leave a great situation for a better one, but this appeared to be leaving for a worse situation. God knew what he was doing, however, and he had things under control. He knew of a ministry opportunity in this desert area. He knows the opportunities that he has for you, too.

Perhaps you don't know what ministry opportunities God has for you. Let me make a practical suggestion. Ask the Lord to provide opportunities for you. Perhaps he already has, and you just haven't noticed. Sometimes we can fail to see that God can use us at our jobs, in our schools, and in some unexpected places and ways. The key is to be willing.

It just so happened that an Ethiopian eunuch was passing by in his chariot. He worked as a treasurer for his queen in Ethiopia and was on his way back from Jerusalem, where he had gone to worship. He was a man searching for God, and the Holy Spirit told Philip to go over to the man's chariot. Philip was a man willing to minister for God.

A second thing we learn from this story is that God provides teachers for our understanding. Philip ran over to the man and heard him reading from a scroll. He was reading aloud from a passage in Isaiah. Philip asked him a simple question, "Do you understand what you are reading?" The Ethiopian responded, "How can I, unless someone guides me?"

I am so thankful that God allows us to be guides. We can have the joy of helping others understand God's word. I am grateful for godly teachers who have helped me by answering my questions or by helping me to grapple with passages of Scripture I didn't understand. Perhaps God wants to use you in such a way. Maybe you could be the one who answers the questions of the co-worker who doesn't understand the Bible or the classmate who has never heard the truth clearly.

The Ethiopian invited Philip to sit with him, and Philip used that opportunity to be a guide to one who was searching and a teacher to one who wanted to learn. Suddenly, the desert became a spiritual classroom.

The third lesson we are taught by the story of Philip and the Ethiopian is that God provides Scripture for verification. The passage the Ethiopian was reading was a passage from Isaiah 53. It referred to a sheep being led to the slaughter; one who was denied justice and whose life was taken away. The man asked the obvious question, "To whom is the prophet referring?"

The Bible tells us that Philip began with that Scripture and told him the good news about Jesus. The whole Bible tells us more about the good news of Jesus. Isaiah prophesied the coming Messiah long before he came and died. Throughout the Old Testament we see God's redemptive plan, fully revealed in the person of his Son, Jesus Christ.

This official knew there was a God from his worship in Jerusalem. Now he knew that God's Son had broken into history. Now he knew that Jesus had died to provide forgiveness for his sin. Now he knew that Jesus had conquered sin, death, and hell through his

We can have the joy of helping others understand God's word.

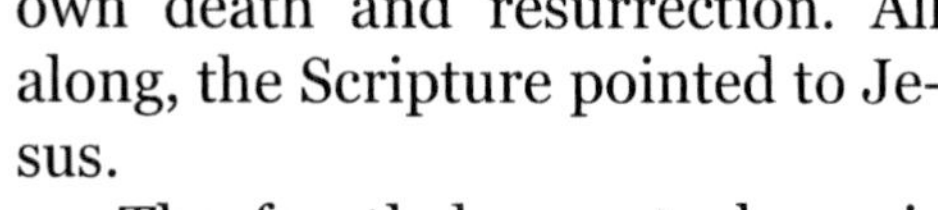

own death and resurrection. All along, the Scripture pointed to Jesus.

Wherever you may find yourself, you will find God willing and able to use you.

The fourth lesson to learn is that God provides opportunities for obedience. After he heard and responded to the message of the gospel, the Ethiopian was ready when God provided an opportunity for obedience. When he saw an oasis in the desert he remarked, "See, here is water! What prevents me from being baptized?"

Following the example of many throughout the book of Acts, the Ethiopian followed the Lord in believer's baptism. As he entered the water with Philip, he apparently became the first of many on the great continent of Africa who would testify to their faith in Christ through baptism. The entourage that undoubtedly accompanied an important man on such a long journey became the first witnesses of God's new work on a new continent.

A fifth lesson we see from this passage is that God provides more opportunities for ministry. You will note that this lesson is suspiciously like the first. The Bible tells us that the Spirit of the Lord carried Philip away and the eunuch saw him no more, though he went on his way to Africa rejoicing. Philip found himself in the region of Azotus. There, he began the cycle of ministry all over again. It didn't matter where the Lord placed him; Philip was looking for opportunities for ministry. And everywhere he went he found those opportunities—in Samaria, in Azotus, on to Caesarea, even in the middle of the desert.

Wherever you may find yourself, you will find God willing and able to use you. Whether the opportunity seems big or small, God will make a difference through you, as you are willing to be used by him. Who knows, maybe God wants to change a continent through you!

Food for Thought

If you are willing, God is able. If you will ask God to provide opportunities for ministry, and be willing to obey his leadership, God will use you to make a difference. The key is your willingness to obey the Lord fully and to follow him wherever he leads.

Faith in Action

Where are you involved in ministry? Think of your spheres of influence—home, job, church, school, community, or neighborhood. What opportunities do you have to share the gospel, serve others, or help someone grow spiritually? Take time to notice the opportunities God has provided you. Write them down and pray over them. Are you willing to step out in obedience so that God can use you to make a difference in your world?

Prayer

Ask God to show you how you can be involved in ministry. Whether the opportunity seems great or small, ask the Lord to use you to make an impact in your world. Ask him to open your eyes to opportunities he may already be providing that you might not have noticed. Ask him to make you willing to be used for his glory.

Learning to See by Going Blind

Acts 9:1-9

Saul rose from the ground, and although his eyes were opened, he saw nothing.
Acts 9:8

After decades of fabulous eyesight I have been reduced to reading glasses. The sharpness of my vision began to slowly fade over time. I noticed that I struggled to see small details. Then, I squinted and strained to see small writing. Finally, I knew I needed help. I got some reading glasses that magnified the letters of books and small details. Suddenly, I could see things I had been missing and now everything is fine. Except now I have a new problem: I can never seem to remember where I placed my glasses!

While glasses, contacts, and eye surgeries are a common part of life, the title of this chapter seems counterintuitive. "Learning to See by Going Blind?" What kind of chapter title is that? Yet this is exactly what happened to a man named Saul. He learned to see by going blind.

The story of Saul (later known as Paul) on the Damascus road is one of the most important stories in the book of Acts. Saul was smart and confident in his standing as a Pharisee, and he was a rising star. He was zealous in his persecution of this strange sect of people who were fol-

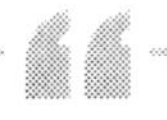

Many who see well physically are blind to the spiritual truths taught in God's word.

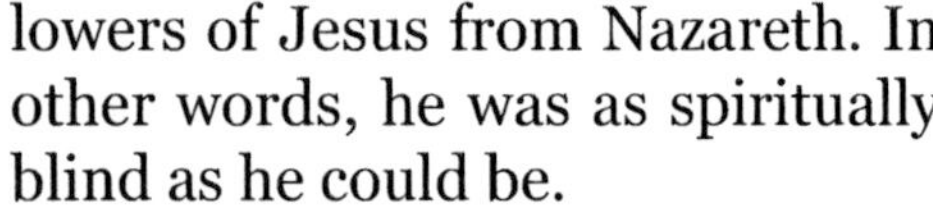

lowers of Jesus from Nazareth. In other words, he was as spiritually blind as he could be.

Saul is not the only one who was cruising through life blind to the truth of the gospel. Many who see well physically are blind to the spiritual truths taught in God's word. Let's note three lessons this story teaches about the spiritually blind and how God can open their eyes.

First, this story teaches us that there is hope for the blind. Who is the very last person you would expect to give their life to Christ? Who is the last one you can imagine repenting of sins and trusting Christ as Savior and Lord? Does someone jump to mind? Is it someone in your family, some jaded co-worker, or that completely worldly guy at the gym?

I suspect Saul was about the last person many would have expected to come to faith in the Lord Jesus. The first verse tells us that Saul was "breathing threats and murder against the disciples of the Lord." Does that sound like someone who is ready to trust Christ as Savior? Verse two says that Saul got permission to go to Damascus to find any followers of the Way and "bring them bound to Jerusalem." Does that sound like imminent salvation to you? No one saw this coming. Saul certainly didn't see it coming, nor did the early believers.

Be careful about giving up on someone too soon. Maybe the Lord is working in ways you can't see. Don't stop praying for that lost relative who has a heart that seems as hard as a brick. Don't stop sharing with that lost friend, boss, or classmate. The artistry of God's painting of salvation is applied to some amazing ways—you know, to stubborn folks like you and me. God can accomplish his work in the lives of people we would never expect. He can break through hard hearts and proud minds in ways that we never anticipate.

Who would have guessed that Saul would end up starting churches all over the place, preaching great sermons to throngs of people, and writing substantial parts of the New Testament? I doubt there were many who saw that happening. But God broke through all of the sinful mess and changed his life, his heart, his direction, and his eternity. God took away Saul's sight so that he could finally see.

A second lesson we learn from this story is that there is a healer for the blind. The Bible tells us that a light from heaven shone around Saul and his sight was gone. Then, he heard a voice from heaven saying, "Saul, Saul, why are you persecuting me (v. 4)?" Saul was so blind that he thought he was persecuting Christians when in actuality he was persecuting Christ. Jesus said, "Truly, I say to you, as you did it to one of the least of these my brothers, you did it to me (Mt 25:40)." Paul thought he was fighting for God when, in actuality, he was fighting against him.

Saul asked what seemed to be a logical question in verse five, "Who are you, Lord?" The answer that followed could not have been more unbelievable to Saul. He heard the words, "I am Jesus." After all, he knew that Jesus was dead; he had been crucified. Sure, he had heard crazy talk from the disciples who said that Jesus was alive, but Saul knew that could not be—until that moment.

Everything Saul thought he knew was in question—his faith, his purpose, his view of life, death, and salvation. Saul thought he could see, and then he discovered that he was actually blind. Fortunately for him and for us, there is a healer for the blind, a sight-giver for the shortsighted. Though we are blind in our lost condition, there is the Great Physician who can give us sight to see truth and eternity.

Be careful about giving up on someone too soon.

The third lesson we are taught through the conversion of Saul is that there is humility for the blind. Saul was a proud man

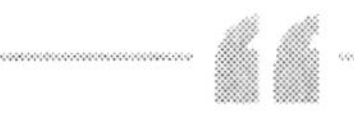

The starting place for salvation is always recognition of our need for God.

who was capable, smart, and ambitious. But there he was, kneeling on the ground in the dirt on the road that led to Damascus. There he was, humbled and blind, needing to be led by another's hand to the city. There he was, with the realization that his life had been empty, meaningless, and a chasing after the wind.

For three days Saul waited there in Damascus. He was blind. He didn't eat, and he didn't drink. And God performed a powerful work in his life. God began to lay the groundwork for the future ministry that he had in store for Saul and for the difficulties that were still to come. For a man accustomed to taking charge, these must have been both perplexing and amazing days.

God did a humbling work in the life of proud Saul. He showed him that he was blind and in need of sight, lost and in need of salvation, weak and in need of a Savior. The starting place for salvation is always recognition of our need for God. We may think we are strong, but we are weak without the Lord. We may think we can see, but we are blind without the vision that only comes from God.

The humbling work of God is not only for salvation. Pride can keep the believer from seeing the truth of his or her need to depend upon God. Pride can keep the believer from tapping into God's power. Pride is just another way of saying that we are blind to the truth of our weakness and blind to our need to trust God completely.

Saul could not see until God took away his sight. And, from that point on, he saw more clearly than ever before.

Food for Thought

We can never see life and eternity as it really is until we see through the lens of the truth of the Lord Jesus. When we begin so see the world and eternity as the Lord sees it, we find our sight more focused than ever before. To see eternity as it really is, we must have vision beyond the earthly to see with spiritual eyes.

Faith in Action

What does it mean to live focused on eternal things? Read 2 Corinthians 4:16-18. It is the ability to invest your life in things that will matter in eternity, things that bring God glory. Too many people invest their time and passions in things that will fade away and things that don't matter in God's kingdom. Stop to evaluate where you are investing your time and passions. Maybe you need to adjust your priorities and focus. Perhaps there is someone you know who needs salvation but seems impossibly far from God. Write down the names of those who come to mind. Pray for them right now and commit to continue to pray for God to move in their lives and to open their eyes to the truth of the gospel. How can God use your testimony and witness in their lives?

Prayer

Ask God to help you see clearly your need for him. Confess any pride that keeps you from seeing God's truth. Pray again for those whom God lays on your heart that need Christ as Savior. Thank God for allowing you to see your need for salvation and for the work he continues to do in your life.

Growing More Capable

Acts 9:19-25

But Saul increased all the more in strength,
and confounded the Jews who lived in Damascus
by proving that Jesus was the Christ.
Acts 9:22

Discipleship is the process of growing deeper and stronger in faith. Never has it been more needed. Shallow faith has become more accepted and more common in the modern world. Many believers act as though salvation is the end rather than the beginning of their faith journey.

The discipleship journey of Saul is instructive. Acts 9 shows us his encounter with Jesus, his realization of his own sinfulness, his turn to Jesus in repentance, and his baptism. But, it shows us something else as well. It shows us a man who grew in discipleship. There are lessons for us to learn about discipleship from the example of Saul. Let's note three discipleship steps in Saul's life that can instruct us regarding discipleship in our own lives.

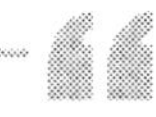

Discipleship is the process of growing deeper and stronger in faith.

First, note the discipleship step of immediate proclamation. Verse 20 is surprising to read.

Evangelism and discipleship go together. They happen simultaneously. We are never to be involved in just discipleship or just evangelism.

The verse tells us that after spending some days with the disciples there in Damascus, "Immediately he proclaimed Jesus in the synagogues." What? He didn't wait for years and years to share his faith? He didn't go through decades of evangelism classes before he began to share his faith with others? What is this "immediately" business?

Please understand two things about the relationship of evangelism and discipleship. First, they go together. They are not opposites, and they are not enemies. They go together like peanut butter and jelly or like chocolate syrup and ice cream. (Are you getting hungry yet?) They are two sides of the same coin of faith. And second, evangelism and discipleship happen simultaneously. We are never to be involved in just discipleship or just evangelism. Both happen together at the same time.

Is basketball about offense or defense? If you know anything about the game, you know that it's about both. Offense and defense are part of the game. Winning teams recognize the importance and value of both. In the same way, the Christian life is about evangelism and discipleship. We must recognize the importance and value of both. The relationship of evangelism and discipleship is such that they must go together. If we are truly growing as disciples we will want to share our faith. If we share our faith we understand the importance of learning and growing in discipleship. They go together.

Saul "immediately" began to share his faith. And, while doing so, he grew as a disciple. The two concepts of evangelism and discipleship are not enemies, but rather twin brothers serving the same goal of honoring the Lord Jesus.

A second discipleship step in Saul's life was growth in knowledge and ability. Verse 22 tells us that Saul "increased all the more in strength" or some translations say he grew more "capable." The idea of this phrase relates to receiving power. It is not that Saul was stronger in his own strength. It is that Saul received the Lord's power to accomplish kingdom work. Saul's increased ability came from his dependence upon the ability given to him by the Lord.

The verse goes on to say that Saul "confounded the Jews who lived in Damascus by proving that Jesus was the Christ." This "confounding" was accomplished through the field of study that we call apologetics. Apologetics is the use of reason, logic, and facts to support the claims of the faith. That rational defense of the faith is vitally important in our current culture.

Fewer and fewer of those growing up in the western world are predisposed towards the Christian faith. The echo of the gospel that was known by their grandparents or great grandparents has grown ever dimmer in the lives of many in our country. They need rational arguments for the legitimacy of the faith.

Saul reasoned with the Jews of Damascus. They knew the prophets but had not understood that the prophets spoke of Jesus. They knew the law but needed to see God's plan of grace for this world full of lawbreakers. Saul used logic and the Old Testament to show them the truth of Jesus the Christ.

One important part of discipleship and evangelism is learning the truth for yourself and then sharing it with others. There are logical reasons to believe the Bible is truly God's word. There are important evidences for the resurrection of Jesus Christ. Many in our world have never been exposed to the evidence and have never truly considered the logical and rational defense of faith. Just as the Lord used Saul to help others see and understand the truth, God can use us to help others ex-

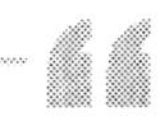

Saul's increased ability came from his dependence upon the ability given to him by the Lord.

Study, learn, and think about the gospel for yourself so that you will be able to help others understand the wonderful truths of the gospel message.

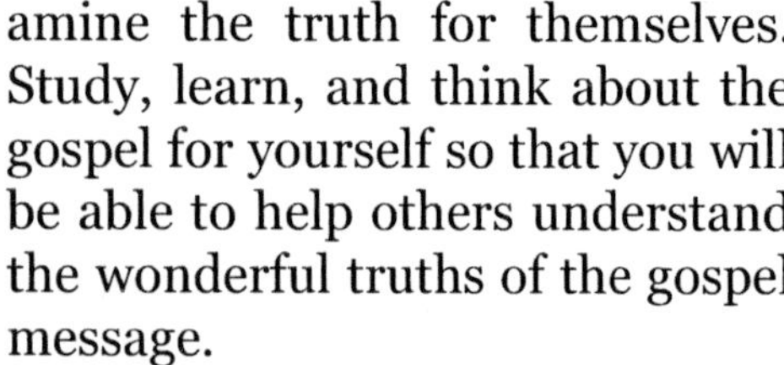

amine the truth for themselves. Study, learn, and think about the gospel for yourself so that you will be able to help others understand the wonderful truths of the gospel message.

The third discipleship step we see in this story is learning to deal with persecution. As is often the case, doing the right thing can lead to difficulties. Saul served the Lord faithfully. But this persecutor turned preacher did great damage to the enemies of the gospel message. They did not like the fact that Saul encouraged others to stop following the Pharisees and other Jewish leaders and to follow Jesus.

The Jewish leaders decided that drastic action had to be taken to stop Saul and the spread of the message of Jesus Christ. So, they plotted to kill him. They watched the gates day and night, looking for an opportunity to put Saul to death.

Word reached the disciples, however. Instead of allowing Saul to be put to death, they found a way around the dilemma. One night, while the Jews watched the gate, they put Saul in a basket and lowered him by ropes through an opening in the city wall. Saul went free, and he continued to grow in his faith and to be used by God in significant ways.

Saul learned some things about difficulties during this experience that are helpful for us to learn as well. He learned that persecution could happen even when you do the right thing. We can serve the Lord faithfully and still have difficulties in this world. In fact, serving the Lord can be hard, challenging, and difficult. He often uses our fellow believers to encourage and help us. He often provides unusual ways of overcoming the problems we face. Most importantly, God always goes with us through the difficulties we face in life.

One of the purposes of this devotional book on Acts is to help you grow deeper as a disciple. God wants you to learn, to follow, and to trust. Whether you are a brand new believer or one who trusted the Lord years ago, I pray that your spiritual strength will increase so that God can use you to make an impact in the world.

We can serve the Lord faithfully and still have difficulties in this world.

Food for Thought

God wants his followers to grow deeper in their faith. Your salvation is a beginning and not an end. The Lord calls you to grow stronger in faith and deeper in understanding. He wants to use you and your witness to help others understand the truth of the gospel.

Faith in Action

If someone asked you to explain your faith in Jesus Christ and why you follow him, could you use reason, logic, and facts to support your claims? What are you currently doing or studying that is helping you grow stronger in your faith and understanding of what you believe? If you need to get stronger in this area, ask your pastor or another committed believer to suggest some resources that will help you. Make a commitment to grow stronger in your faith. Another way to grow stronger is through sharing your faith with others. Look for opportunities to help others see the truth of the gospel and the trustworthiness of his word and plan. Are you going through a difficult time in your life because of your faith? Allow God to use this difficulty to strengthen you and to bring glory to his name through it.

Prayer

Ask the Lord to deepen your faith and strengthen your witness. Ask him to help you to be a bold witness even when facing difficult times or challenges. Ask him to help you to become the disciple that he wants you to be.

No Common Man

Acts 10:9-33

Now therefore we are all here in the presence of God to hear all that you have been commanded by the Lord.
Acts 10:33

As a young man, I naively thought racial animosity and prejudice would be virtually eradicated by the time I was an adult. But that animosity and prejudice is as old as the hills, and we continue to see it today. The enemy is really effective at dividing us by our differences. Even the body of Christ is often divided by race, age, and preference.

In the days of the early church, there was great prejudice between the Jews and the Gentiles. Many Jews had forgotten that God's covenant promise with Abraham extended to all nations (Gen 12:1-3). They began to see God as exclusive to the Jewish nation and often looked down on the Gentiles as virtually unredeemable. Those prejudices festered, simmered, and led to strife and bitterness. And it continues to this day.

This backdrop brings us to the powerful story found in Acts 10. Two characters dominate the story. One is a Gentile named Cornelius who is described as a devout man who feared God and was involved in many charitable acts. Though he did not fully understand God, he prayed to him and sought to know him. He lived as a centurion of the Roman army. He was a soldier, a leader, and a seeker of

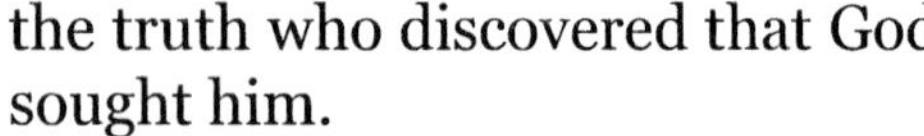

Many Jews had forgotten that God's covenant promise with Abraham extended to all nations.

the truth who discovered that God sought him.

The other man is Simon Peter. Peter was an apostle of Jesus and served as a leader in the fledgling church. He was Jewish, devout, and serious about his faith in Christ. But it was hard for him to imagine, given his cultural baggage, that God was serious about the salvation of the Gentiles.

Each man had a vision and each was destined to learn important truths through their encounter. Cornelius had a vision of an angel who told him that God had heard his prayers and seen his acts. He told him to send men to Joppa where they would find a man named Simon Peter who would talk to him about the truth.

Peter had a vision of a great sheet coming down from heaven. On the sheet were all kinds of animals and a voice told him to eat them. Peter, however, refused because those animals were unclean. The voice replied, "What God has made clean, do not call common." This vision was played out three times and left Peter perplexed. And, just as he wondered what all this meant, the men sent by Cornelius showed up at the door of the home where Peter was staying. Suddenly, Peter understood what God was trying to teach him.

The visions were not just for Peter and Cornelius. They were recorded for our benefit as well. The story teaches us three important lessons that we need to discover today, just as they did long ago.

The first lesson to note from this passage is that every life has value. Like many Jewish men, it was hard for Peter to understand the great value of Gentile life. But every life has value before God. We are created in the image of God and that gives us tremendous value. The death of Jesus on the cross reinforces the incredible value God places on human life. Peter said in verse 28, "God has shown me that I should not call any person common or unclean."

I read a book recently on the life of Thomas Jefferson. He wrote such stirring words in my country's Declaration of Independence about how everyone is endowed by the Creator with certain inalienable rights, which included liberty. Oddly, the man who penned those stirring words wrote them even as his slaves labored outside his window.

Jefferson was a walking contradiction. He spoke of the rights of freedom yet held men in bondage. It is the same mindset that leads to the devaluing of life today through racism and our modern scourge of abortion. Our society continues to devalue life, and it shows in our actions and attitudes.

God used the vision in the life of Peter to show him that every life has value. The lives of those Jewish apostles were of great value because they had been created by God and then redeemed by the blood of Jesus. Peter discovered that the life of a Gentile centurion, and by extension, of all Gentiles had great value; they too were created in God's image and could experience the saving work of the Lord Jesus on their behalf. Peter preached Christ and him crucified to these eager Gentiles who listened and discovered salvation for themselves.

A second lesson to be learned from these verses is that every life has potential. Perhaps Peter never imagined the potential to impact the cause of Christ that could be found in a single Roman soldier. Cornelius had not grown up in the Jewish traditions. He had not sat at the feet of Jesus as he taught. He had not been given the same opportunities afforded Peter. But Cornelius, like all people, had tremendous potential in Christ.

The death of Jesus on the cross reinforces the incredible value God places on human life.

God doesn't just see what you are; he sees what you can be. Just as the Lord saw something in the obscure fisherman named Peter, he saw something in the Ro-

God doesn't just see what you are; he sees what you can be.

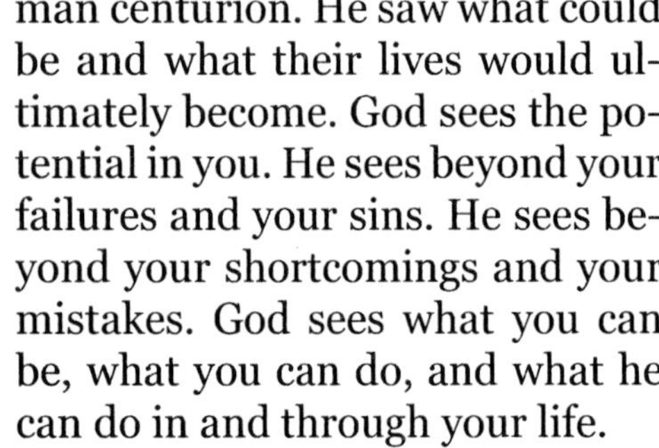

man centurion. He saw what could be and what their lives would ultimately become. God sees the potential in you. He sees beyond your failures and your sins. He sees beyond your shortcomings and your mistakes. God sees what you can be, what you can do, and what he can do in and through your life.

The third lesson we are taught by this story is that every life has opportunity. Just as the Lord provided an opportunity for Peter, he provided an opportunity for Cornelius. And, that opportunity came through Peter. The man who saw Gentiles as beyond the scope of grace discovered that God wanted to use him to lead a Gentile to the source of grace.

Perhaps God wants to use you to provide someone with the opportunity to hear the message of the gospel. Maybe God wants you to reach across generational lines to share with someone older or younger. Maybe God wants to you to reach across racial lines to share with someone. Maybe God wants to use you to go on a mission trip to a faraway place to share the message of the gospel. Or perhaps he has brought the world to your doorstep so that you can cross cultural barriers right across the street. After all, God has shown you that you should not call any person common or unclean.

Food for Thought

God cares about people of every nation, tongue, and tribe. The enemy wants to erect barriers to keep us from sharing God's love with anyone who is in any way "different" than us. But God cares about people of all cultures, backgrounds, and needs. As you come to recognize and embrace the value of others, God can use you to help others come to know his love.

Faith in Action

Try to be completely honest with yourself and ask yourself these questions. Do you ever find yourself hesitant to help or reach out to someone of a different race? Or a different lifestyle? Or a different culture? If this is true for you, evaluate why. As you meet people from all walks of life today, be intentional about reminding yourself that every person has value, potential, and the opportunity to know God. In fact, he might want to use you. Look for opportunities to be involved for the cause of Christ. Are you willing to cross cultural and other barriers for the sake of the gospel? Consider going on a mission trip, or supporting someone else if you are unable to go.

Prayer

Ask God to help you value others as he values them. Ask him to provide you with opportunities to be an influence for the cause of Christ. Ask the Lord to help you and your church to be willing and intentional in crossing barriers erected by the enemy so that all can discover his grace.

Even the Gentiles

Acts 11:1-18

And the Spirit told me to go with them, making no distinction.
Acts 11:12

News of Peter's encounter with Cornelius swept through the early church. Many were surprised to hear that Peter was sharing the message of the gospel with those who weren't Jewish, and they confronted Peter upon his return to Jerusalem. "Why would you go to eat with Gentiles?" they demanded. Like Peter previously believed, they did not envision the message of the gospel extending to everyone, and certainly not to uncircumcised Gentiles like this Roman centurion. Wasn't God's salvation only for the Jews? Could God really care about others?

Peter used the occasion to tell them the entire vision he had received from the Lord and how God had opened his mind to overcome his prejudices. He told of the sheet that came down from heaven and the voice that told him to eat and said, "What God has made clean do not call common." He told of the Spirit's leadership telling him to go to Cornelius' home, and told them of the Holy Spirit who fell on the Gentiles as they trusted Christ as Savior.

This passage teaches us three lessons about our attitudes that we would do well to learn. Our attitude towards others is a reflection of our understanding of God and his plan. Note these lessons from Acts 11.

Our attitude towards others is a reflection of our understanding of God and his plan.

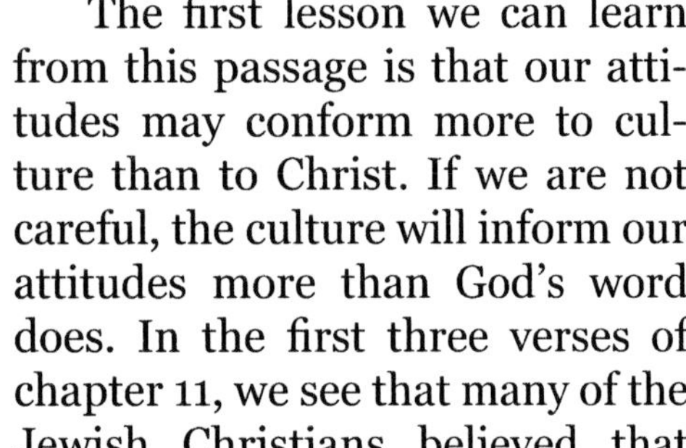

The first lesson we can learn from this passage is that our attitudes may conform more to culture than to Christ. If we are not careful, the culture will inform our attitudes more than God's word does. In the first three verses of chapter 11, we see that many of the Jewish Christians believed that salvation was only for the Jews. That is, many of them still worked under the false assumption that Christianity was only for those who were Jews. They failed to see that God had a plan for the whole world to know him—people of every race, tribe, and tongue.

Culture is a powerful force. It can shape us in ways that we hardly notice. Because we live in it every day, we can find ourselves shaped by it without realizing what has happened. The first two verses of Romans 12 tell us not to be conformed to the world but to be transformed by Christ. The world is always working to conform us. Our culture is trying to mold us and shape us into its own image.

If you have ever played with play dough (And if you have never done so, please find your inner child and play with some today!), you know how easy it is to conform it to the pressure of your fingers. You can easily roll it into a ball, my personal favorite, or into a skinny snake. You conform the play dough by the pressure you put on it; it is an easy thing to do.

Culture can be a pressure similar to that. It pushes against you and tries to shape you. It presses you in ways that you hardly notice. The songs and the movies of our culture are always trying to mold us to see the world in a certain way. They press against us every day. "Love is just a feeling that can't be controlled," the songs of our generation tell us. "Personal pleasure is what matters most," shouts our movies. If we aren't careful, we may find our attitudes and actions shaped more by the culture around us than by the plans God has given to us.

The Bible tells us to follow a different path. We are to be transformed. We are to follow Christ rather than culture. We are to follow God's plan rather than the world's plan. We can recognize the pressures of the world and choose to stand against those forces. We can choose to follow God's plans and purposes and to see the world as God sees it. The transformed life is a life that chooses to obey God's direction rather than the world's suggestion.

Peter and many other Jewish Christians were in danger of allowing their own prejudices to inform them more than God's eternal plan. But when Peter saw that the Holy Spirit came to Cornelius and his friends, he understood that God's plan of salvation extended to all who would repent and believe. There was a powerful change in his understanding of God's plan and that led to a transformed attitude towards others.

A second lesson to learn from this passage is that our attitude can hinder God's work in our lives. Peter spoke powerful words in verse 17. He said, "If then God gave the same gift to them as he gave to us when we believed in the Lord Jesus Christ, who was I that I could stand in God's way?" Peter realized that he had been in danger of standing in God's way. The man who had committed himself to be a disciple of the Lord was in danger of standing in his Lord's way.

Our attitudes can hinder the work of God in our lives. Certainly God can work around us. But our wrong attitudes can keep God from doing his work through us. We can actually find ourselves standing in the way of what God is doing in the world and in us. Our wrong attitudes can hinder God's work instead of help it.

> *"The transformed life is a life that chooses to obey God's direction rather than the world's suggestion."*

1 Thessalonians 5:19 tells us, "Do not quench the Spirit." Wrong attitudes can quench God's Spirit and his work in our lives. Ephesians 4:30 says, "And do not grieve the Holy Spirit of God."

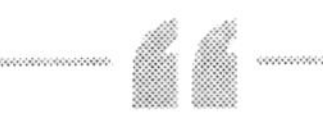

God can work around us. But our wrong attitudes can keep God from doing his work through us.

Wrong attitudes are a means by which we can cause grief to the Holy Spirit and hinder his work in us. We could say it like this. Our attitudes go a long way in determining whether we are productive in God's kingdom or whether we are a hindrance to the work of God's kingdom.

A third lesson to learn from this passage is that our attitude can change to reflect God's perspective. Peter's witness and new understanding had a powerful impact on the other Jewish believers. Verse 18 records the change. "When they heard these things they fell silent. And they glorified God, saying, 'Then to the Gentiles also God has granted repentance that leads to life.'"

We don't have to live with wrong attitudes or cultural blinders. We can overcome the prejudices and biases of culture and history by God's Spirit. We can find new unity and fellowship. God can change hearts and open minds. God can help us to see life as he sees it rather than how culture views it.

When we understand God's great love for people we can begin to love them in the same way he loves them. We can discover that God's family includes people of every race, tongue, and tribe. And, we can be used by God to make a difference in the world in a way that honors his name now and forever.

Food for Thought *God wants us to be aware of the conforming pressure of our culture and world. Instead of being conformed to the world, we are to be conformed to his image. We can allow him to transform the way that we think and act. Old prejudices and faulty perceptions can melt away as we begin to see the world as the Lord sees it and love as the Lord loves.*

Faith in Action *Review your answers from yesterday's Action Step. Consider the ways in which your past, your culture, and the conforming pressures of the world have kept you from seeing things and people as God sees them. What steps will you take to begin to build relationships with believers and unbelievers of different ages, races, and cultural backgrounds so that you can discover the unity that comes through faith in Jesus Christ? What areas of your life are you knowingly or unknowingly allowing the world to conform your thoughts and actions? Take a quick spiritual inventory and ask God to reveal those areas to you.*

Prayer *Ask the Lord to keep you from the dangers of materialism, hedonism, racism, or other cultural pressures that would hinder you from living with a God-centered faith. Instead, ask the Lord to help you live a transformed life where you follow him fully and completely. Ask the Lord to open your eyes to opportunities to share the gospel with others. Pray for churches and missionaries serving among different cultures around the world. Pray for your own church that it will welcome all people and be faithful to proclaim God's good news for everyone.*

Do Prayers Get Answered?

Acts 12:12-17

They said to her, "You are out of your mind."
Acts 12:15

The great English preacher Charles Spurgeon once spoke with a discouraged pastor. The pastor was discouraged by the lack of response to his sermons. Spurgeon said to the young man, "You don't really expect response every time you preach, do you?" "No," the young man responded, "I guess I don't." "Then that is exactly why you don't have it," Spurgeon declared.

Do we really expect God to answer our prayers? Do we really believe that he is able to answer what we ask of him and do what we ask him to do? Is it possible that we can pray and not expect God to work or to answer?

What an odd phenomena! Apparently, we can ask the Lord to do something without really believing he can do it. We can pray without expecting God to answer. We can seek without truly expecting to find. Even the early church struggled with this problem.

Prayer isn't to be our last resort; it is to be our first response.

Acts 12:12-17

God can do his work without our prayers. But God wants us to join him in his work through prayer.

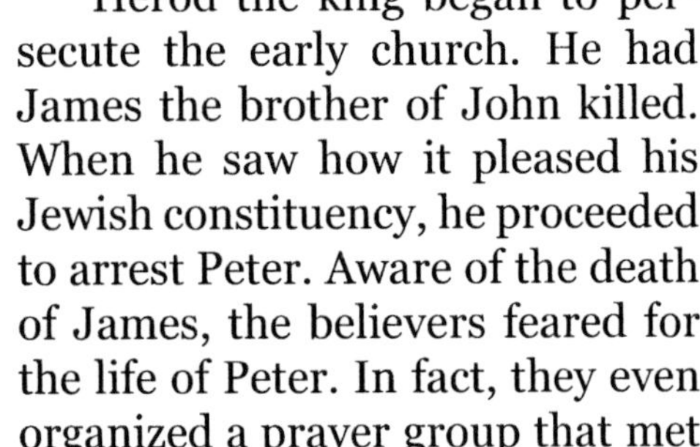

Herod the king began to persecute the early church. He had James the brother of John killed. When he saw how it pleased his Jewish constituency, he proceeded to arrest Peter. Aware of the death of James, the believers feared for the life of Peter. In fact, they even organized a prayer group that met in the home of Mary, the mother of John Mark. Many gathered and prayed earnestly. But then the strangest thing happened—God answered their prayers!

At the very time the church was gathered in the home of Mary to pray for Peter, God sent an angel to release Peter from his prison cell. The angel led Peter past all the gates and the guards and into freedom. Peter, fresh out of jail, went to the home where the church was gathered to pray for him and knocked at the door. The people were so busy praying for Peter's release that they did not notice his knock. Eventually, a young servant girl named Rhoda heard the knock and asked who was there. She was amazed at what she heard.

Recognizing Peter's voice, Rhoda was overjoyed. But instead of opening the gate, she ran to the gathered supplicants and informed them that the object of their prayers stood at the door. And what was their response? "You are out of your mind," some said. "It is his angel," concluded another. They prayed for Peter to be delivered but did not believe that their prayers had led to his delivery. What an odd response. Have you ever been praying but not believing? It seems to be a common story.

But Peter kept knocking and knocking. Finally, someone decided they should see who knocked so persistently. There was Peter, delivered and free. Their prayers had been answered—and they were shocked. May I suggest the obvious? There was a connection between the prayers of the people for Peter and the delivery God provided for Peter. There is a connection between our prayers and the work God wants to do in us and through us in this world. God wants us to pray because prayer is critical to the work of God in our lives and circumstances.

Let's note five things about prayer as we contemplate this story. First, see that prayer is the natural response of the needy heart. It is natural for us to pray when we have a need. In fact, prayer should be our first response. It isn't to be our last resort; it is to be our first response.

I heard of a church that was having some serious problems. After much deliberation, someone in the church suggested they take the time to pray about the issues. "Oh no," came the response, "has it come to that? Is it really that serious?" Prayer for believers should always be our first response to any need in our lives. Prayer will become increasingly important and urgent in our lives the more often we make it our first response.

You may be in a season of earnest prayer right now because of some serious need in your life or the life of a loved one. Prayer is vitally important to you at this moment. If you are not in a time of need at this time, just wait. If you live long enough you will have moments when you recognize your great need of reaching out to the Lord in prayer.

Second, see that prayer reaches to the very heart of heaven. I know that God can do his work without our prayers. But God wants us to join him in his work through prayer. Prayer touches the heart of God. He longs for us to invite him into our problems, needs, and difficulties. God desires the connection he has with us when we pray.

Could God have delivered Peter from prison without the prayers of the church? Of course he could. But God delivered him in response to the prayers of those believers. There is something about prayer that gets to the heart of our connection and our relationship to the Lord. Nothing can

Prayer is not an afterthought to God's work; it is God's work.

> *Prayer is the power plant of the Christian life and no other activity can generate the spiritual energy necessary to live the life God wants for his followers.*

replace the intimacy with the Lord we experience through prayer.

Third, see that when we pray we are involved in God's will and work. Prayer is the work of the Christian. Prayer is the work of the church. Through prayer we are involved in seeking God's will, and we are involved in the work God is doing in the world.

The early church was serious about prayer. We see them praying earnestly and faithfully. Prayer is not an afterthought to God's work; it is God's work. Prayer is rolling up our spiritual sleeves and engaging in the spiritual work of God.

Fourth, see that prayer is a powerful tool. There is power in prayer. James 5:16 states, "The prayer of a righteous person has great power as it is working." Notice that this verse describes prayer from a righteous person as having "great power." There is a power that comes through prayer that will be experienced in no other way.

Do you want power in your Christian life? Pray. Do you want power in the life of your ministry? Pray. Do you want power in your Bible study class and in your church? Pray. There is power for the Christian life that is found in no other place than the prayer closet. There is a strength that is found in no other posture than on your knees. Prayer is the power plant of the Christian life and no other activity can generate the spiritual energy necessary to live the life God wants for his followers. But that power can be found in only one source—prayer.

Fifth, see that prayer is a worthy endeavor. Would you make prayer more than a brief habit before a meal or at a church service? Instead, make it an active part of your life. I suggest you begin each day with a dedicated period of time in prayer. Pray for your needs and the needs of others. Praise the Lord in prayer. Confess your sins and shortcomings in prayer. Pray for wisdom and discernment.

Prayer is worthy of your time, your energy, and your commitment. And, who knows? Maybe the Lord will answer your prayers as he did the prayers of the group gathered in the home of Mary long ago. Remember, while you are praying, be sure to listen for the sound of a knocking door!

Food for Thought

Prayer is an important part of the work of God. The Lord answered the prayers of the early church on behalf of Peter even though they did not expect him to work as he did. There is a power to prayer and a value in prayer. Prayer needs to be an integral part of the life of everyone who calls on the name of the Lord. Through prayer, God involves us in his work in the world.

Faith in Action

Begin a serious and dedicated approach to prayer. This week, spend time in specific prayer for yourself and for others. I recommend that you use a prayer journal to write down the names of people you want to pray for. Write down specific needs and concerns for yourself and others. Spend time praising the Lord. Make confession a part of your prayer time. And don't forget to listen.

Prayer

Ask the Lord to teach you to pray. Ask him to help you to see the value and importance of prayer. Ask the Lord to increase your love of prayer and to increase your faith as you pray. Ask him to help you to make this important practice of prayer a permanent part of your life.

Local Church—Global Work

Acts 13:1-3

Then after fasting and praying they laid their hands on them and sent them off.
Acts 13:3

A preacher told a story about a pastor he knew. He said the man was the pastor of a small church in the mountains of North Carolina and had a radio ministry on the tiny FM radio station in his small town. Though the station did not carry more than a couple of miles through those hills, the pastor began each of his broadcasts with the words, "Hello world." The preacher who told the story saw it as a humorous example of pastoral hubris. But I wonder if that mountain preacher didn't have it more correct than we know. Our local churches can have a huge and lasting impact upon this world. Even a small local church has the ability to change the world by the power of God.

Acts 13 reminds us of the importance of the local church. It shows us the value, the importance, and the power of the church, and what the church can do when following the Lord fully. Let's note three lessons to be learned from these three verses in Acts 13. Each of them can help us to understand more of God's plan for the church and for the world.

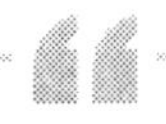

We need the strength that comes from being a part of the larger body of believers, and we need the lessons of faith that are best learned in a shared community of faith.

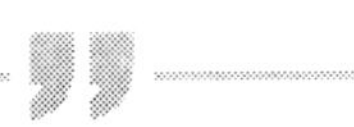

First, this passage teaches us that every Christian has a church. Notice that verse one speaks of the church at Antioch. These were the gathered Christians in that city who met together to worship, witness, to grow in discipleship, and to minister to others. They gathered to fellowship and to glorify the Lord. They were the church.

There are two different ways that we can speak of the church. There is the entire body of Christ throughout the world and throughout the ages that makes up the universal church. Every believer has a connection with all other believers who know Christ as Savior. We are in the same family and a part of the same body. Together, we are the universal church.

There is, however, another sense of the church. It is the local church—the church in Antioch, the church in Jerusalem, the church in O'Fallon, Illinois, or the church in your community. The local church has great importance to the work of Christ and great value for the believer.

Every believer needs to be part of a local church. We need the fellowship and connection that comes with the church. We need the strength that comes from being a part of the larger body of believers, and we need the lessons of faith that are best learned in a shared community of faith. But many believers have failed to see the great value of this entity.

An anti-local church mindset began in the 1960's and 1970's. "Down with the establishment" was the cry of a young generation; and that attitude spilled over to the church. "We don't want to be part of organized religion," some Christians said. Others said, "We like Jesus, but we don't like the church." However, Jesus himself formed the church and is its chief Cornerstone.

The generation that was against the local church lost something important. With the loss of connection came the loss of accountability, encouragement, and power. With the loss of the local church came a loss of the strength and support that comes through our work with other believers. We need each other. We need the church.

I want to urge you to get actively involved in a local church. And, since I am asking something of you already, take it another step and get actively involved in a small group within your local church. The church is a "God thing," and God formed it for a reason.

A second lesson to be learned from this passage is that every Christian has a role within the church. Notice that those in the church at Antioch had different gifts. There were prophets and there were teachers. The church is described as a body in Romans 12 and 1 Corinthians 12. Just like a human body with different parts and functions, every believer in a church body is different yet working together for the same goal of honoring the Lord.

Notice that those in the church at Antioch had different backgrounds. One of the men, Manaen, was a lifelong friend of Herod the tetrarch. He had political connections. Another was from Cyrene, a city in North Africa. Barnabas and Saul were there with their unique backgrounds as well.

One of the things I love about the church where I serve as pastor is the wide variety of backgrounds, talents, and gifts represented. Partly because of our close proximity to a large Air Force base, we have people from every part of the nation in our church. We even have quite a number who grew up in a different country. We have different races, cultural backgrounds, and talents in our church. It makes our worship and fellowship all the more rich and sweet.

> *With all of our differences, there is a binding unity that comes through our commitment to the same Lord and Savior.*

Although the church has different gifts and backgrounds,

He desires for your local church to have a global impact.

we do have a common purpose. We are different, but we are unified. We are unified with our purpose of bringing glory to God. We are unified in our purpose of pointing others to salvation in the Lord Jesus Christ. We are unified in our worship of the one who is worthy of our worship. With all of our differences, there is a binding unity that comes through our commitment to the same Lord and Savior.

May I note how much your role in your local church matters? Your church can never be all that she could be without you. Perhaps you don't think your contribution to the body of Christ is significant at all. Perhaps you think of yourself as the little pinky toe in the body of Christ and that you matter as much as a pinky toe matters.

The other night I got up out of bed to go to the bathroom. It was dark, I was sleepy, and I didn't see it coming. But I stubbed my pinky toe on the side of the bed. It was terrible! I writhed in pain and woke everyone in the family. The hurt of that little toe kept me from walking properly for the next couple of days. Don't tell me the pinky toe doesn't matter—and don't tell me that you don't matter to your church. God made you and saved you for a reason. Get connected to the church. God has a role for you.

The third lesson we are taught by these verses is that every church has a calling. God wanted to use the church at Antioch in a way that went far beyond their region. He has global work for your church as well. He desires for your local church to have a global impact.

It is worth noting that the church is called out of worship. Verse two says, "While they were worshiping the Lord and fasting, the Holy Spirit said, 'Set apart for me Barnabas and Saul for the work to which I have called them.'" As the church worshiped and fasted, they heard from God. God wanted their local worship to lead to worship in regions far away.

The church is also called to witness. The work to which Barnabas and Saul were called was missionary work. These two men journeyed to many places where they shared the gospel and started churches with people of other cultures. In verse three we see that the church at Antioch took their role of support seriously. They fasted, prayed, and laid their hands on the men. Then, they sent them off on their missionary journey.

Our local churches can participate in God's work in other places and with other cultures just like the church at Antioch did. We can go on mission trips and share the message of the gospel. God may even want some of us to be missionaries like Paul and Barnabas. Or, we can support those from among us who are called to leave their homes and serve as missionaries in faraway places. We "hold the ropes" for those who are called and sent. Your church matters. It is local, but it has a global work. Your church should be making an impact right where you are, but it should also be making an impact to the ends of the earth. The church truly is a "God thing."

Food for Thought

The church has tremendous value and the ability to make a significant impact in the world. The local church can extend its impact beyond a local region and impact the world through missions. Every member of a church has a role to play that is vitally important. Whether your role is to go to the ends of the earth or to be the support for those who do, you can participate in God's worldwide plan for the church.

Faith in Action

Take a moment to write down the ways that you are participating in your church's mission. Are you serving, giving, praying, or even going into your community to make an impact for the gospel? Have you ever considered going on a mission trip? If you aren't already, get active in your local church. Connect with others in a small group. Find out the gifts and abilities that God has given to you and how you might use them to make a difference in and through your local church. Consider going on a mission trip or increasing your support of career missionaries.

Prayer

Ask the Lord to do a powerful work through your local church. Pray for the leaders of your church by name. Ask the Lord to use your church to make a lasting impact locally and internationally. Pray for missionaries who are serving in other countries and ask the Lord to show you ways that you can support them.

The Trouble with Discipleship

Acts 14:21-28

And they remained no little time with the disciples.
Acts 14:28

Do you want to know the trouble with discipleship? It takes hard work. It takes some rolling up of the metaphorical sleeves and some blood, sweat, and tears. But discipleship is worth it.

The goal of the gospel is committed discipleship. God wants us to become fully committed and fully devoted followers of him. That is what discipleship is all about. Discipleship is about personal growth toward a lifestyle of following the Lord at all times and in every area of your life.

Let me tell you how important discipleship was to the early church. Paul preached, taught, evangelized, and started churches. Then, after he experienced conflict with Jewish authorities, Paul faced persecution. Paul got stoned—in the biblical sense of the word. That, my friend, was a bad day. In pain and left for dead, Paul laid on the side of the road. But his Christian brothers gathered around him and prayed for him. Paul found the supernatural strength to get up and go on.

Discipleship is about personal growth toward a lifestyle of following the Lord at all times and in every area of your life.

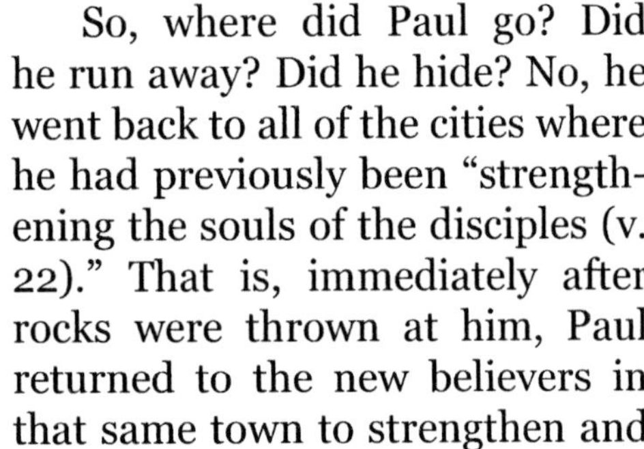

So, where did Paul go? Did he run away? Did he hide? No, he went back to all of the cities where he had previously been "strengthening the souls of the disciples (v. 22)." That is, immediately after rocks were thrown at him, Paul returned to the new believers in that same town to strengthen and deepen their faith. He continued the process of discipleship.

In today's text, Paul and Barnabas reveal six things that are necessary for the hard work of discipleship. These six aspects of discipleship remind us of what it takes to make committed followers of Christ.

First, discipleship takes encouragement. Verse 21 tells us that after Paul and Barnabas preached the gospel in Derbe, where many trusted Christ for salvation, they returned to the cities they had visited previously. They returned to Iconium, Antioch, and to Lystra, the very city where Paul was stoned earlier. The Bible tells us in verse 22 that they spoke to the believers "encouraging them to continue in the faith."

Encouragement is so important to the faith because discouragement is so common to the faith. These believers in the early church faced persecution, hardship, and difficulties. They could have easily grown discouraged. But Paul and Barnabas went to great lengths to encourage them. They talked to them about the kingdom of God and the big picture. They spoke with them about the reality of difficulties in this world. And they pointed them to the encouragement that comes from genuine faith.

Barnabas is one of my favorite Bible characters. Virtually every time he is mentioned in the Bible he is encouraging someone. His name even means "son of encouragement." This guy knew the value and benefit of encouragement. We need people like Barnabas today. Maybe you could be that encouraging friend to some fellow believer today.

Second, discipleship takes perseverance. Paul and Barnabas told these new believers "that through many tribulations we must enter the kingdom of God (v. 22)." There was no sugar coating of Christianity for these folks; they were told the hard truth. This is a fallen world, and there will be difficulties and tribulations. But we must go through these valleys, not be defeated by them. We must stay on the path even when it grows narrow and steep. Perseverance is one of the most important aspects of discipleship. We stick with it when things are tough. We stay faithful though the road is hard. "Persevere!" the Lord commands.

Have you ever quit a diet? Ever quit an exercise program? Ever start to learn a language but quit about a week into it? Quitting is easy and common. Discipleship demands perseverance and endurance. The Bible implores us to stick with it despite the overwhelming problems. Paul urges us to continue on despite the certain tribulations.

Third, discipleship takes community. Verse 23 states that Paul and Barnabas appointed elders in every church and committed them to the Lord. That is, they helped the church to organize and prepare for effectiveness.

There is no better tool for discipleship than the local church. The church is God's idea and God's design. Through it we gain community, fellowship, accountability, and strength. The early Christians formed churches so that the gospel would take deep roots and communities of believers could find critical fellowship. Truth is, we need each other. We need a community, we need a family, and we need connection. That is what the local church is all about.

Encouragement is so important to the faith because discouragement is so common to the faith.

Fourth, discipleship takes consistency. Verses 21-26 list eight

Discipleship is not a onetime deal. It is a lifelong process.

cities or regions where Paul and Barnabas retraced their steps and stopped a second time. They were not just concerned with an initial visit where people would hear the gospel message. Paul and Barnabas were concerned with continued growth in those churches and among those believers. They visited a second time and encouraged continued spiritual development.

Discipleship is not a onetime deal. It is a lifelong process. It is about a consistent and continuous walk with the Lord Jesus Christ. It is about taking up your cross daily and following him. It is about understanding the importance of reading the Bible consistently and praying without ceasing. It is about walking for a long time in the same direction following the Lord. Consistency matters.

Fifth, discipleship takes communication. Verse 27 tells of these missionary church planters preaching again. They "declared all that God had done with them, and how he had opened a door of faith to the Gentiles." The early church was always preaching, teaching, and communicating the truth of the gospel. They spoke about it often and communicated the truth at every opportunity. They never took lightly the importance of teaching the truth of God. Effective teaching is a vital part of effective discipleship.

Sixth, and finally, discipleship takes time. Verse 28 states, "And they remained no little time with the disciples." Isn't that a beautiful verse? They spent time in developing disciples. They devoted the necessary time to teaching and training.

Mushrooms spring up overnight. Oak trees take a while. But what a difference in the strength of these two plants. Discipleship takes time. One might even say that discipleship takes a lifetime. But the strength and impact of a life that grows deep spiritual roots is worth all the effort and all the trouble.

Food for Thought

God wants us to grow in our discipleship. And, he wants us to help others grow in their faith as well. Discipleship takes effort but is well worth it. Perhaps God wants to use you to help others grow in their faith just as he is growing you in your faith. God can use you to encourage and strengthen others on their journey of faith.

Faith in Action

What steps are you taking to grow in your personal discipleship? You cannot help others grow unless you have a vibrant, growing faith of your own. Be faithful in Bible reading, prayer, worship, and witness. Seek to put into practice the lessons of God's word. Write down steps that you will take to continue your personal growth. Are you actively involved in helping other believers to grow in their faith? There are ministries through your local church where you can be involved in the discipleship of others. If you aren't involved in one, ask your church leaders where you might help. More immediately, look for a specific way today to encourage another believer in their faith journey.

Prayer

Ask God for the strength and endurance to help you do the hard work of discipleship and spiritual growth. Ask him for the perseverance to be consistent in your own spiritual life even through tribulations. Ask the Lord to show you opportunities to help other believers grow in their walk with Christ as well.

Dealing with Controversy

Acts 15:1-11

But we believe that we will be saved through the grace of the Lord Jesus, just as they will.
Acts 15:11

Controversy is no stranger to Christianity. There have been arguments, disagreements, and controversies regarding faith since the establishment of the church. Jesus himself was considered quite controversial in his day and is still a controversial figure in our generation. But the controversy described in Acts 15 threatened to tear apart the early church.

The way that Paul, Barnabas, Peter, and the leaders of the early church dealt with this controversy is very instructive for us in dealing with controversy today. There are three principles that we see in this text that can help us deal with controversy in the right way.

First, note that controversy is to be dealt with proportionately. Not all controversies are equal. Some people make controversies out of everything. Others fear conflict so much that they are unwilling to confront any issue. But, there ought to be a sense of proportion as we deal with controversy.

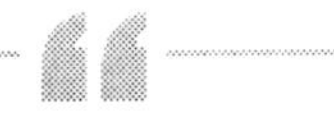

We don't have to take a stand on every preference or every fad. But there are some controversies where we must take a stand.

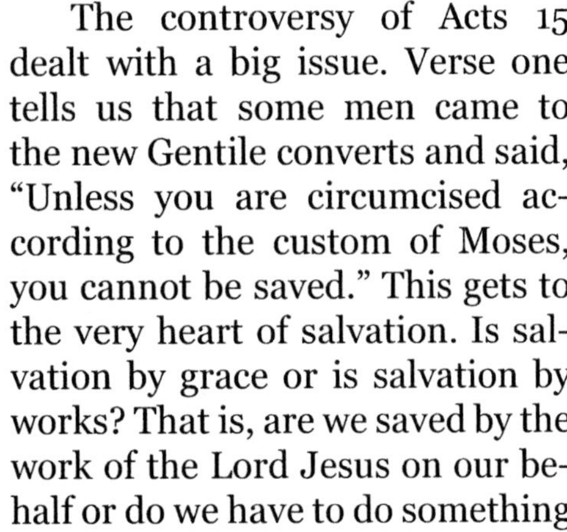

The controversy of Acts 15 dealt with a big issue. Verse one tells us that some men came to the new Gentile converts and said, "Unless you are circumcised according to the custom of Moses, you cannot be saved." This gets to the very heart of salvation. Is salvation by grace or is salvation by works? That is, are we saved by the work of the Lord Jesus on our behalf or do we have to do something in addition to that work to be saved? This was a critical and central question to be answered by the early church.

Verses four and five tell us that Paul and Barnabas considered this issue to be so important that they brought it to the church leaders in Jerusalem. There the church leaders began to grapple with the question. Some Pharisees who came to Christ said, "It is necessary to circumcise them and to order them to keep the Law of Moses." Grace was not enough, this group said. They argued that Gentile believers needed grace and circumcision; in other words, they needed grace and the law.

Paul, Barnabas, and Peter saw this as a battle worth fighting. They stood vigorously on the side of grace and willingly fought this war. This was definitely a hill on which to die for these men. However, not every controversy is a hill on which to die. We don't have to take a stand on every preference or every fad. But there are some controversies where we must take a stand.

Think of the Lone Ranger when you think about what stands to take. The Lone Ranger had silver bullets. Silver bullets were hard to get and expensive to make. You don't go around popping off shots at every tin can that you see if you have silver bullets. You save those for the really important moments. The Lone Ranger was careful about pulling his trigger.

Not every issue of life is worthy of taking a non-negotiable stand. If you are always fighting it might say more about your contentious spirit than your principled commitments. But if you never fight it might say something about your courage or lack thereof. There are some battles worth fighting. And the battle over the nature of salvation was one such battle.

I was in seminary when the battle over the nature of the Bible was raging in the Southern Baptist Convention. I believed then, as I do now, that it was worth taking a stand on the inerrancy of the Bible. Taking that stand did not always make me popular, but I believe that stand made me right. Don't fight just to fight, but realize that there are some battles worth engaging.

A second thing to note is that controversy is to be dealt with appropriately. Paul and Barnabas dealt with the controversy over the nature of salvation in a couple of ways. The first thing they did is described in verse two. They "had no small dissension and debate with them." Paul and Barnabas engaged those saying circumcision was required for salvation in vigorous debate and discussion. The seriousness of the argument is emphasized with the word "dissension."

Not only did they argue with those teaching incorrectly, they also engaged the larger church family and the leadership in the discussion. They wanted the church as a whole to deal correctly with this issue. They understood the value of involving the church in Jerusalem along with the apostles and elders in such a critical issue. It was a wise and correct way of dealing with a controversy that had the potential to tear the early church apart.

"If you are always fighting it might say more about your contentious spirit than your principled commitments. But if you never fight it might say something about your courage or lack thereof."

There are appropriate and inappropriate ways to deal with controversy and disagreement in general. Being hateful or vindic-

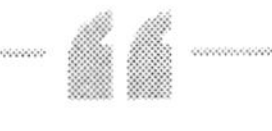

> *Being right does not give one the freedom to be unkind.*

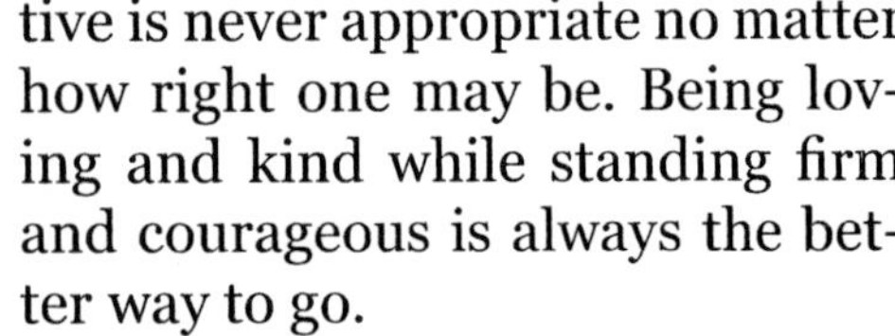

tive is never appropriate no matter how right one may be. Being loving and kind while standing firm and courageous is always the better way to go.

I mentioned that I stood for the inerrancy of Scripture during the controversy that raged during my seminary years and beyond. I tried to take a principled stand while being kind to those with whom I disagreed. While I don't know that I always met this standard, I wanted to be charitable with those who saw the issues differently than I did. But I also wanted to be unwavering on what I believed to be the correct and biblical view. Being right does not give one the freedom to be unkind.

The third principle to recognize from this text is that controversy is to be dealt with directly. Paul and Barnabas made their case for salvation by grace alone before the apostles and elders. Others argued that salvation required the keeping of the law and circumcision. Peter, however, stood tall at this moment. Peter recounted how God had chosen him as the means by which Cornelius and other Gentiles heard the message of the gospel. He noted how the Holy Spirit came to them confirming the legitimacy of their salvation. He explained how God "made no distinction between us and them, having cleansed their hearts by faith (v. 9)."

Peter reminded them that no one had kept the law fully. Not one of them in the room had been able to fully meet the requirements of the law. That very fact caused them to recognize that they were sinners, and they needed what only God could do for them. They needed Christ to pay the debt because they were helpless to pay it.

Peter closed his argument with these powerful words in verse 11. "But we believe that we will be saved through the grace of the Lord Jesus, just as they will be." He emphasized that the Jewish Christians were saved by

God's grace alone and not by their works. And, he noted that the same would be true of any Gentile Christians. They would be saved by God's grace alone and not by circumcision, the keeping of the law, or any other good works.

Controversy has been around forever and will, I suppose, be with us until the return of Christ. Learning to deal with controversy proportionately, appropriately, and directly can keep us on track as we deal with disagreements. And, it can help us to go forward into the unified future that God has for us as we follow his will completely. May God grant us a principled unity.

Food for Thought

The Lord wants us to deal with controversy in a way that honors him. That means we don't fight just to fight, and we don't run from battles that must be fought. Learning to deal with controversy proportionately, appropriately, and directly can keep us on target for dealing with these issues in the right way and with the right spirit.

Faith in Action

How would you describe yourself? Do you have a contentious spirit that always looks for a fight or disagreement? Or, do you have a fearful spirit that is never willing to stand for truth? Think of a particular controversy or issue in your life where you disagree with someone. Evaluate how you are handling it in relation to what you read today. Stand for truth in a kind and loving way. Love those with whom you disagree. Seek counsel and guidance from trustworthy believers.

Prayer

Ask the Lord to give you a firm but loving spirit. Ask him to help you to choose to stand for the right things and to do so with the right spirit. Ask him to give you a commitment to the truth so that you stand for the right things and a commitment to respect so that you stand in the right way.

Open Doors

Acts 16:6-10

And a vision appeared to Paul in the night: a man of Macedonia was standing there, urging him and saying, "Come over to Macedonia and help us."
Acts 16:9

I had my life all planned out as a boy. I was going to save up $1,000. At 16, I would try out for the St. Louis Cardinals baseball team and be immediately signed, of course. Then, I would move on to a career as a successful major league baseball player. Only it didn't work out like I planned. God shut some doors—I couldn't hit a curveball, and I wasn't really that good against a fastball. Oh, and I fell far short of my $1,000 goal! God opened some doors—I had a clear but shocking call to preach! My plans were changed as God opened and closed doors of opportunity for me.

Paul, Silas, and a young man named Timothy went on a missionary journey. But the journey did not go as they expected. There were some twists and turns as God used circumstances to direct their path. Let's note three principles about how God uses open and closed doors to direct our journeys.

First, note that God closes some surprising doors. The Bible tells us that this missionary team of Paul, Silas, and Timothy found themselves in the region of Phrygia and Galatia because they were unable to go into Asia as

God has a ministry for you. But not every ministry is for you.

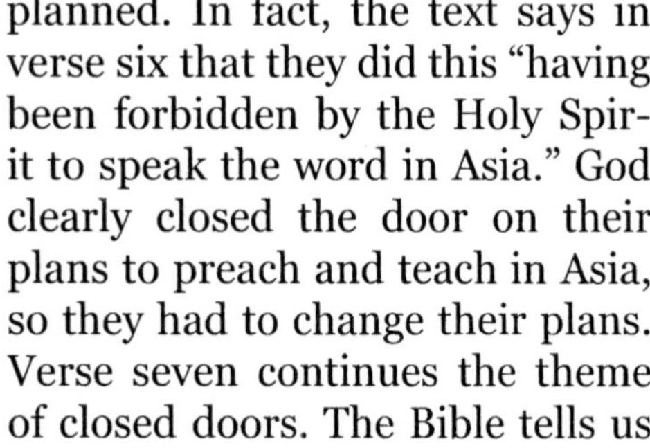

planned. In fact, the text says in verse six that they did this "having been forbidden by the Holy Spirit to speak the word in Asia." God clearly closed the door on their plans to preach and teach in Asia, so they had to change their plans. Verse seven continues the theme of closed doors. The Bible tells us that the team went to Mysia and then attempted to go into Bithynia, "But the Spirit of Jesus did not allow them." A second door was closed, and their plans had to be changed again.

I want to suggest three words that will help you to deal with God's leading as he shuts and opens doors of opportunity for you. The three words are tenderness, task, and timing.

The word tenderness reminds us to be sensitive to God's leading. God's plans are more important than our plans. God knows the future, so he leads in ways we might not anticipate. Wise is the follower who remains sensitive to his guidance. Beware of your heart growing hard by following your own plans. Instead, have a heart that is tender towards what God wants you to do.

The word task is a reminder that God has a *ministry* for you. But not every ministry is *for* you. Someone needed to take the gospel to Asia, but that task wasn't for Paul, Silas, and Timothy. Someone needed to take the gospel to Bithynia, but that task wasn't for this group. You can't do everything. God has a task for you that is unique, important, and personal. You are responsible for the task God has for you and not for the task he has for someone else.

The word timing reminds us that sometimes God's timing is different than ours. The timing of obedience can be as important as the task of obedience. God sometimes shuts doors because it isn't the right time for us to enter that door. God's timing may lead to closed doors that will open later.

I wonder if the mission team was a bit frustrated at these closed doors. After all, taking the gospel to these places was a good and noble thing. But God knows what he is doing. He knows the needs and the opportunities in ways that we can't know. As a result, God closes some surprising doors.

Second, closed doors can lead us to open doors. The door to Bithynia was closed, so the team moved on to Troas. It was there that Paul had a vision. Verse nine describes the vision, "A man of Macedonia was standing there, urging him and saying, 'Come over to Macedonia and help us.'"

God had closed the door to Asia and Bithynia because he had opened the door to Macedonia. I speculate that something like this might have happened. A man in Macedonia had been seeking to know God, but no one around him knew God well enough to explain the truth to him. He began to pray, "God, I want to know you. There is a void in my life, and I know you are real. Every time I look into the night sky the stars are a witness of your greatness. Would you send someone to show me the truth of who you are?" I think God answered that prayer and sent this vision to Paul so that he would follow this open door of opportunity.

God shuts some doors only to open others. He limits opportunities in one area only to expand opportunities in others. Closed doors can be frustrating unless we acknowledge that God uses them to reveal the open door opportunities he has planned for us.

> *Closed doors can be frustrating unless we acknowledge that God uses them to reveal the open door opportunities he has planned for us.*

I have been the pastor of First Baptist Church of O'Fallon, Illinois, for 20 years. It is a great ministry, and I love the church

dearly. It is exactly the fit God had for me. But before I came here all those years ago, a really good church talked to me about being their pastor. It seemed like a great fit and a great opportunity. But God clearly shut the door. I was surprised, but God unmistakably spoke to my heart that I was not to go there. And then, just a short time later, God clearly opened the door to go to O'Fallon. He shut one door only to open another that led exactly where he wanted me to be.

Third, open doors are opportunities for effectiveness. Open doors are ministry opportunities. After seeing the vision of the man in Macedonia, Paul knew what God was doing. Verse 10 states, "Immediately we sought to go into Macedonia, concluding that God had called us to preach the gospel to them."

It was clear to Paul and the group. God wanted them to go to Macedonia; so they went. God called them, and they obeyed. And God made them highly effective in Macedonia as the truth of the gospel took root and the message thrived. Many came to faith in Christ, multiple churches were planted, and the work of the kingdom of God expanded. God was at work through open and closed doors, and he was at work in unexpected ways and places.

God provides opportunities for us to minister for his glory. He uses his word and circumstances to show us what he wants us to do and where he wants us to be. I pray you will be willing to follow the Lord as he opens and shuts doors to lead you exactly where he wants you to be and to do exactly what he wants you to do.

Food for Thought

God has a plan and purpose for your life. He will use circumstances to help you to see what he wants you to do. Sometimes he will close doors of opportunity so that he can lead you through other open doors of opportunity. Remain sensitive to his leading in a daily walk with him through prayer and Bible study. As you do this, God will direct you to the ministry opportunities he has planned for you in just the right place at just the right time.

Faith in Action

Look back and identify some times in your life when God shut the door on your plans. Were you able to acknowledge that he knows best? Were you able to see another door of opportunity open to you? Thank him for how he guided your steps. Renew your commitment to being open to what God wants for you. Look for opportunities where you are right now to minister to others in Jesus name. Be open to opportunities God may have for you in the future.

Prayer

Ask the Lord to give you clear direction on what he wants you to do. Trust him that he will. Thank him for closing doors in your life that weren't his best for you, and commit to be willing to obey his leading by following the open doors of opportunity that he provides for you. Ask the Lord to use you in a way that honors his name and leaves a lasting impact for his glory.

Examining the Scriptures

Acts 17:10-15

They received the word with all eagerness, examining the Scriptures daily to see if these things were so.
Acts 17:11b

Church names can be strangely interesting. I knew a church called Little Hope Church. It was located in a community known as Little Hope; hence the name. At least, I hope it was named after the community. I've driven by Halfway Baptist Church on many occasions. If it is halfway Baptist, I wonder what the other half is!

There are many churches named Corinth Baptist or Corinth Methodist or Corinth whatever. Corinth was probably the most dysfunctional church in the New Testament. Did the founders of these churches not know that, or were they foretelling their own future? I was the pastor of First Baptist Church of Corinth, Texas for ten years. We were named after the town and not the dysfunctional New Testament church, I am happy to say.

While I cannot fully understand all church names, I do understand those who use the name Berea. The church at Berea, described in Acts 17, was an amazing place, and I want us to note four characteristics of this thriving New Testament church.

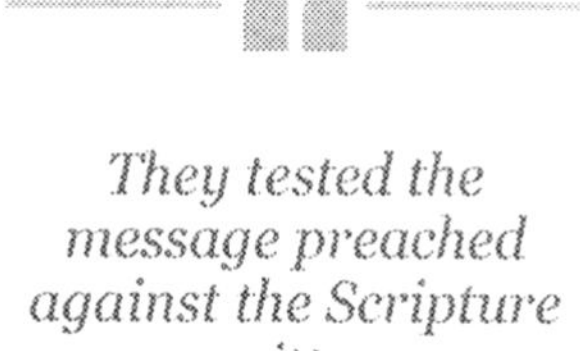

They tested the message preached against the Scripture written.

First, note that the church at Berea was engaged in scriptural examination. Upon arriving in Berea, Paul and Silas followed their customary pattern by going into the synagogue and talking to the Jews about the gospel message. The Jews in Thessalonica had not received the message well. But the Bible tells us something interesting about the character of the Jews in Berea. They were "more noble" than the Jews in Thessalonica (v. 11).

This verse tells us that the Bereans "received the word with all eagerness, examining the Scriptures daily to see if these things were so." They didn't just ignore the message delivered by Paul and Silas, nor did they simply accept it without question. They examined the Scriptures carefully to see if the message preached was true to God's word.

I love this about the people of Berea. They tested the message preached against the Scripture written. They studied the Bible to test the accuracy of the word spoken to them by Paul and Silas. Perhaps this is why modern churches sometimes name themselves after this city. This is a group that showed discernment and was serious about God's word.

Discernment is greatly needed in our generation. We need Christians who study God's word for themselves. We need to examine teaching and preaching through the lens of God's perfect word. We must discern if what is taught lines up with Scripture. By doing so, we can know the truth and the truth can set us free.

Second, note that the church at Berea had spiritual enthusiasm. There was an eagerness to study the word and compare it to the preaching of the gospel. I love that word "eagerness." It implies that the Bereans wanted to find the truth and were excited about the search. The message of the gospel being preached by Paul and Silas told of God's plans to forgive sins. They were eager to discover that message. The gospel preached proclaimed that God sent his son to pay the penalty for sins on the cross. They were eager to learn about that sacrificial love. And, the message preached told of Jesus conquering sin, death, and hell through the resurrection. The Berean Christians were eager to find and claim that victory.

I love to see eagerness and enthusiasm for God's word. Unfortunately, it isn't always evident in the lives of Christians and churches. Some make the Bible seem dull, dry, and boring instead of alive, vibrant, and exciting. Some see studying God's word as a duty instead of a privilege. How sad!

Years ago, I was the guest preacher in a church out of state. I arrived at church early, so I decided to attend a Sunday School class. It was a small church, and there was only one option. So, I walked into the room and sat down. No one knew me or that I was preaching the sermon in the next hour.

The teacher, an older woman, began the class by stating how much the lesson was like the previous couple of lessons. She said that it didn't make much sense to study lessons that were so similar. But, she guessed that they would go ahead and work through the lesson anyway—not a great start. What I soon discovered was that this would be the high point of the class. The class that day made God's word seem as dry and irrelevant as it could possibly be. It was as dull and boring as reading from a phone book. That class totally missed the point that God's word is alive, vibrant, dynamic, and incredibly relevant.

We need eagerness in our study of God's word. We need enthusiasm for the things that count. There should be some excitement about the great opportunity the Lord gives us to study the Scrip-

Adversity can come even when God is working in a church, but God's work is greater.

tures ourselves and with others. The church at Berea understood this truth.

Third, note the steady expansion of the church at Berea. Verse 12 tells us, "Many of them therefore believed." Their study confirmed the trustworthiness and the truthfulness of the gospel message. Many responded by placing their faith in Jesus Christ as Lord and Savior.

Not only did many Jews respond in faith, but Gentiles did as well. The Bible tells us that many Greeks, both men and women, came to faith in Christ. And, many of the women came from positions of influence within the city. The fledgling church of Berea began to thrive as men and women, Jews and Greeks, placed their trust in Jesus and began to follow him.

I love it when my lost friends begin to look into the faith. When they do, they discover the trustworthiness of God's word and the truth of the gospel message. They find a firm foundation for faith and discover that faith stands the rigors of intellectual study. When they begin to examine the Scriptures for themselves, they find the powerful truth of a God who intervenes in human history and has provided a means for our forgiveness and salvation.

Fourth, note that the church at Berea had serious encounters. Along with the great expansion of the church came great adversity. The Jews at Thessalonica came to Berea and began to agitate and stir up the crowds. The adversity grew great enough that Paul left to go to other ministry opportunities. Silas and Timothy, however, stayed to encourage and strengthen this young and growing congregation.

Adversity can come even when God is working in a church. We should never be entirely surprised that the enemy hates to see God's work thriving, and that he will seek to bring disunity, adversity, and difficulty. But God's work is greater and can thrive even during difficult times. The Bereans understood this truth. After all, they searched God's word and saw it for themselves.

Food for Thought

There is power in searching God's word. When we read and study the Bible for ourselves, we find truth and discernment. As the people of Berea searched the Scriptures they discovered the truth of God's work and plan. It led them to believe the message of the gospel and to trust Jesus with their lives and future. God's word is powerful and teaches us to know and understand the truth and to live our lives according to God's plan and purpose.

Faith in Action

Ask yourself these questions and evaluate where you need to change. What is your attitude about studying God's word? Do you consider it a great privilege and an exciting responsibility? Or, do you find it a tiresome task or duty? Do you prefer to be spoon-fed, listening to someone else tell you what the Bible says? Or, do you have a desire to get into the word and see for yourself? The teaching and preaching of God's word is important, but it should not take the place of individual and personal study. The impact of a truth learned and confirmed through personal discovery is life changing.

Prayer

Ask God to birth in you a desire to study his word. Pray that the Lord will give you a renewed enthusiasm for the study of the Scriptures. Ask the Lord to help you to be faithful in your personal study of the Bible so that you will know the truth of God's word and be able to discern right from wrong. Thank God for his life-changing word written, preserved, and given to you so that you can know him and his purposes for you.

An Unknown God

Acts 17:22-34

The God who made the world and everything in it, being Lord of heaven and earth, does not live in temples made by man, nor is he served by human hands, as though he needed anything, since he himself gives to all mankind life and breath and everything.
Acts 17:24-25

It was one of the most famous cities of the ancient world. Athens was the center of philosophical discussion and intellectual pursuit. Though the Romans had supplanted the Greeks as the great political power of the day, Athens was still a major center of the cultural world. But Paul could not help but notice the spiritual darkness of the city. It was filled with idols, yet the people lacked an understanding of the one, true God. As was his usual custom, Paul reasoned with the inhabitants of the city, both the Jews and the Greeks.

After hearing his initial discourse, the Epicurean and Stoic philosophers took him to the Areopagus, the center of discussion and philosophical discourse. Verse 21 describes the Athenians and foreigners who lived in Athens as people who spent "their time in nothing except telling and hearing something new." They lived to ponder and debate new ideas.

Paul, of course, used the occasion to preach the message of the gospel. Through that sermon he taught

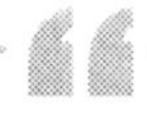

Religion, wrongly practiced, is simply man's attempt to reach or appease God on his own merit.

the gathered intellectuals the truth about God and his plans for mankind. There are six particular truths Paul taught.

The first lesson Paul taught the gathered Athenians was that God wants more from us than religion. As Paul began his sermon at the Areopagus, he noted that they were "very religious (v. 22)." He observed the large number of idols and noted that they even had an altar "to the unknown god." Proof was everywhere that the people were very religious; they acknowledged many gods. However, they did not know the one, true God who had revealed himself to his creation.

Religion, however devout, is not enough. If religion was enough, Paul could have remained a Pharisee. Religion, wrongly practiced, is simply man's attempt to reach or appease God on his own merit. The Athenians even wanted to appease an unknown god they might have missed in their polytheistic practices. But the problem with attempting to appease God is highlighted in these questions. How much is enough? How much must we do? How perfect must we be?

The gospel reminds us that we are all sinners. No amount of good works or reform can erase that fact. Even if we were capable of living perfectly from this point forward what hope is there of overcoming the sins we have already committed? Heaven is perfect, and we certainly aren't.

The message of the gospel is that we can't be saved by religious practices. We must trust that Christ has done for us what we cannot do for ourselves—pay our sin debt. We must trust his righteousness and not our own. Once we accept the message of the gospel and trust Christ as our Savior, he will begin to transform our hearts. We may participate in religious activities such as worship, service, and prayer, but religious activities are our response to God's work in us, not a replacement for God's work.

A second lesson taught by Paul was that God is great and not dependent upon us. In verses 24-26, Paul makes the argument that God created the world and everything in it. He cannot be contained in temples, and he does not need human works for his purposes to be accomplished. He needs nothing from us. He is great and powerful—the Lord of heaven and earth.

Like many in our day, the Athenians failed to see the greatness and power of God. Many see God as weak and unable to accomplish anything, if they see him at all. Some may see him as a nice old man who is loving but powerless to do much. Yet, the God portrayed in the Bible is all-powerful and all knowing. He is bigger than our world and our universe. He is bigger than our needs and our problems.

A third lesson that Paul taught was that God can be known by man. What a surprising concept this must have been for the philosophers of Athens. Their gods were distant. Paul spoke of the one true God as close, intimate, and personal. In verse 27 he said that God "is actually not far from each one of us." God created the universe, and he continues to be actively involved in it. He is not distant, but close.

There was a time when Deism was a popular philosophy in our country. The idea of the Deist is that God created the universe but then withdrew from it. He made us but isn't actively involved with us. However, the Bible portrays God quite differently. God broke into this world through the person of Jesus Christ. God became man and lived among us, taught us, and gave his life for us. He is not a distant God. He is the God who desires to know us and be known by us.

God desires to know us and be known by us.

A fourth lesson that Paul proclaimed to the Athenians was

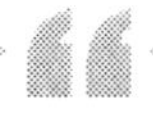

There is power in the testimony of believers whose lives have been made new by their encounter with the risen King.

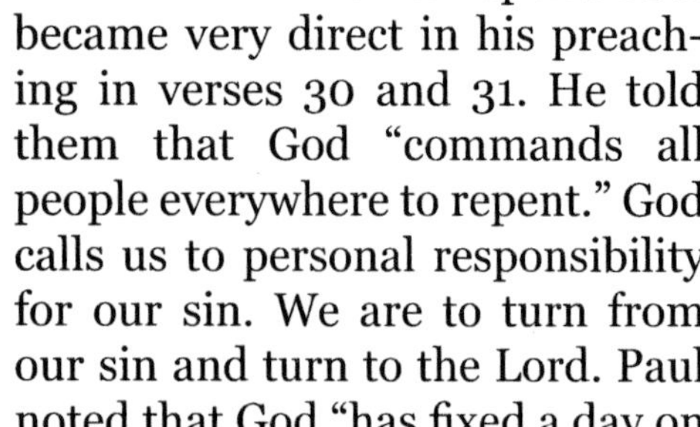

that God calls men to repent. Paul became very direct in his preaching in verses 30 and 31. He told them that God "commands all people everywhere to repent." God calls us to personal responsibility for our sin. We are to turn from our sin and turn to the Lord. Paul noted that God "has fixed a day on which he will judge the world." God is a righteous judge, and we will all stand before him one day.

A fifth truth Paul preached at the Areopagus was that God provides evidence of the resurrection of Jesus. He said in verse 31 that the world was to be judged "by a man whom he has appointed; and of this he has given assurance to all by raising him from the dead." This reference to the resurrection of Jesus Christ was mocked by many of the philosophers, because dead men stay dead.

Then, as now, the resurrection is critical to our faith. If Jesus did not rise from the dead our faith is in vain. But if he did rise from the dead, he is indeed the one who conquered the power of sin and hell. If he did rise from the dead, there is hope for humanity.

Paul gave evidence of the resurrection through the testimony of those who saw Jesus alive. And, he gave testimony of the resurrection by the transformed lives of those who had trusted Jesus as Savior. Paul's own life was radically transformed by his meeting with the risen Savior. There is power in the testimony of believers whose lives have been made new by their encounter with the risen King.

A sixth lesson taught by Paul was that God can be known through faith. While many scoffed at the notion that Jesus was crucified and raised from the dead, others believed. Some men and women in Athens placed their faith in Jesus Christ and found salvation full and free by his blood.

The gospel is powerful. When we believe in Jesus we find forgiveness and new life. These men and women in Athens discovered something more powerful than religion. They discovered something more powerful than philosophy and education. They discovered the transforming power of a personal relationship with the God of the universe. They discovered the God who can be known.

Food for Thought

God is unknown to many in our world. They don't know who he is or what he has done. But God can be known. He has revealed himself to us in his word and through his son, Jesus Christ. We are saved when we repent of our sins and place our faith in Jesus, the one who died for us and rose from the dead. We can know God as our Savior and our Lord. We can have more than empty, futile religion; we can have a relationship with the God who made the universe.

Faith in Action

Do you know anyone who believes that there is a God but doesn't know him personally? Do you know anyone who has an incorrect view of God? Look again at the six truths taught through Paul's message in our passage. Pray and plan for a way to share these truths with that person.

Prayer

Ask the Lord to empower you to be a faithful witness to others. Ask the Lord to use you where you are to help others discover a relationship with him. Pray specifically for the person you thought of in the Action Step. Ask the Lord to use you to help make him known to the nations. Commit to help his name be proclaimed to the ends of the earth. Ask the Lord to use you in missions to reach those who have never heard. Pray for missionaries who share the gospel in places where people have never heard of the one, true God. Ask the Lord to use you and your church beyond your church walls to have an impact among the nations.

Occupied with the Word

Acts 18:5-11

And the Lord said to Paul one night in a vision, "Do not be afraid, but go on speaking and do not be silent, for I am with you"
Acts 18:9-10

I love preaching. I know not everyone can say that, but I can. Some find preaching boring, irrelevant, and a waste of time; I hate that. Though my own preaching has not always had the kind of impact I wanted, I know that preaching is something that comes from the Lord. He calls people to preach, and therefore it should be something that is important, meaningful, and prioritized.

When I was a young preacher, having been a pastor for only a short time, I heard a man give a stinging critique of the preaching of Adrian Rogers. Rogers was the long time pastor of Bellevue Baptist Church in Memphis, Tennessee, and I thought he was about the best preacher I had ever heard. I remember thinking to myself, "If there are folks who don't like the preaching of Adrian Rogers, what hope do I have?" Regardless of ability, preaching was something God called me to do, and I have taken it seriously. I don't take myself too seriously, but I take my ministry seriously.

Preaching was at the heart of God's methodology for spreading the gospel.

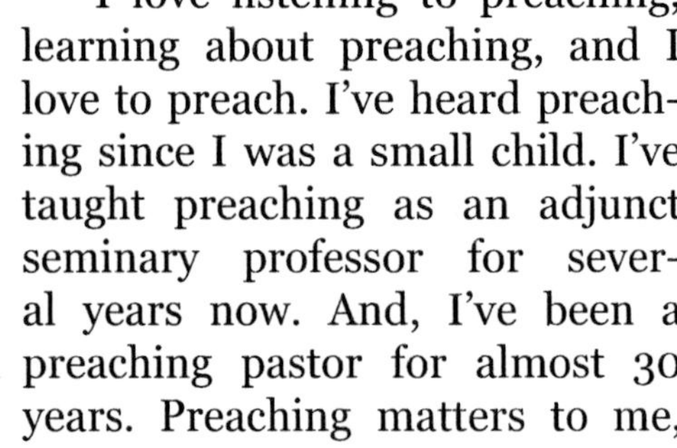

I love listening to preaching, learning about preaching, and I love to preach. I've heard preaching since I was a small child. I've taught preaching as an adjunct seminary professor for several years now. And, I've been a preaching pastor for almost 30 years. Preaching matters to me, and preaching should matter to you.

In Acts 18 we find Paul in the city of Corinth. Silas and Timothy joined him there, and the Bible says, "Paul was occupied with the word, testifying to the Jews that the Christ was Jesus (v. 5)." Paul was proclaiming the message of the gospel to the Jews in Corinth. In other words, Paul was preaching. That is what Paul did—he proclaimed publicly the message of salvation.

This passage teaches us four things about preaching. Perhaps these elements will remind us of the importance of the preaching.

First, these verses speak to the priority of preaching. Verse five, along with many places in the New Testament, demonstrates a high view of preaching. Paul was "occupied" with the word. Preaching was something that took energy, time, and commitment.

Preaching was central in the New Testament. It was at the heart of God's methodology for spreading the gospel. 2 Timothy 4:1-2 records Paul's words to his younger associate. He said, "I charge you in the presence of God and of Christ Jesus, who is to judge the living and the dead, and by his appearing and his kingdom: preach the word; be ready in season and out of season; reprove, rebuke, and exhort, with complete patience and teaching." Paul gave a strong charge to Timothy: Preach the word.

Preaching in the New Testament was also careful. Note that Paul was occupied with "the word." He was preaching God's message and not his own. Paul said in 1 Corinthians 1:17, "For Christ did not send me to baptize but to preach the gospel, and not with words of eloquent wisdom, lest the cross of Christ be emptied of its power." The message of preaching is to be God's word. It is not our cleverness, ability, or wisdom that people need; they need God's word.

Preaching in the New Testament was critical. It was the preaching of the most important message the world would ever hear—the gospel of Jesus Christ. Paul said in 1 Corinthians 1:23-24, "We preach Christ crucified, a stumbling block to Jews and folly to Gentiles, but to those who are called, both Jews and Greeks, Christ the power of God and the wisdom of God." The message of the gospel is the critical need for this lost world.

Second, these verses speak to the problem of preaching. As hard as this is to believe, not everyone listens to the message. Some will tune out, some will day dream, some will doodle, and some will listen but never allow the truth to penetrate beyond their ears.

But, it gets worse than that. In verse six, the Bible tells us that some "opposed and reviled" Paul. They didn't just nap in disinterest during his preaching. They stood in opposition to the message of God's word. That same reaction seems to be gaining traction in our own time and culture. It seems that more and more people are not just ignoring God's word; they are opposing God's word.

Paul responded to the opposition by shaking out his garments; a symbolic gesture that he was done with them. He declared as much to them in verse six, "Your blood be on your own heads! I am innocent. From now on I will go to the Gentiles." Ultimately, the preacher has the responsibility to preach the truth with boldness and passion. But he does so knowing that some will ignore him and others may even oppose him.

Third, these verses speak to the purpose of preaching. Not everyone opposed the message of the

It is not our cleverness, ability, or wisdom that people need; they need God's word.

The preacher has the responsibility to preach the truth with boldness and passion. But some will ignore him and others may even oppose him.

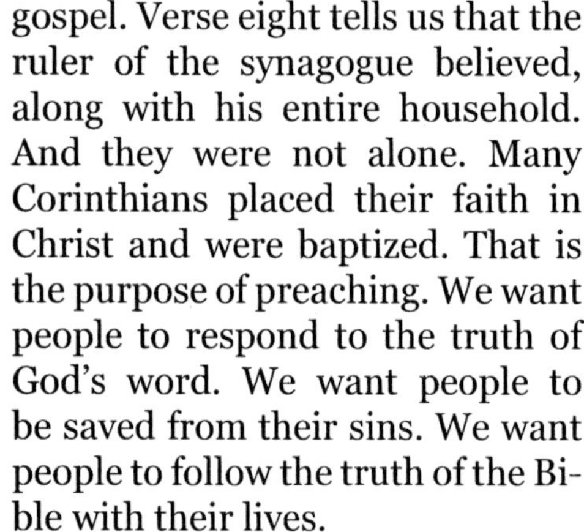

gospel. Verse eight tells us that the ruler of the synagogue believed, along with his entire household. And they were not alone. Many Corinthians placed their faith in Christ and were baptized. That is the purpose of preaching. We want people to respond to the truth of God's word. We want people to be saved from their sins. We want people to follow the truth of the Bible with their lives.

Having been a pastor for a long time, I have seen my share of people ignore God's word. But I am so delighted when I see people respond to God's word by trusting Christ as Savior and following him as Lord. I love to see that happen. On many occasions through the years I have seen God work through the simple preaching of the word to change lives. I never get tired of seeing people follow the Lord Jesus in baptism. I never tire of seeing people grow in their faith and blossom in their commitment to Christ. It is always the goal of my preaching.

Fourth, these verses speak to the power of preaching. Verse 11 tells us that Paul stayed a year and a half in Corinth "teaching the word of God among them." There is power in God's word. We preach God's word because it has the power to transform hearts and change lives. People need more than our opinions. They need the power that comes from the word of God; they need the power that comes from the gospel message; they need teachers and preachers who are occupied with God's word and who will preach God's truth to them.

We preach God's word because it has the power to transform hearts and change lives.

Food for Thought

The word of God is powerful and life changing. God uses the proclamation of his word to transform lives through salvation and spiritual development. Bible teachers who study God's word faithfully and teach God's word passionately can be used by God to change lives and eternity. God always blesses the careful, clear proclamation of his word.

Faith in Action

Read Romans 1:16 and Hebrews 4:12. If you are a Bible teacher or preacher, you have been reminded today that any transforming power in your preaching or teaching comes from the proclamation of God's word. Recommit yourself to teaching God's word effectively. Study God's word faithfully, and proclaim his word passionately. To those who sit under Bible teachers and preachers, approach each sermon or lesson with an understanding and appreciation of the importance of the proclamation of God's word. Each time you listen, make a practice of asking God to make you a good hearer of the word by putting into practice the truths that you learn.

Prayer

Pray for those who teach and preach in your church. Ask the Lord to empower their study and their preparation. Ask the Lord to give them great passion for his word and great enthusiasm for teaching it clearly and carefully. And ask the Lord to make you a receptive listener. Pray that you will receive God's powerful word and allow it to transform your heart and life.

The Lord's Will

Acts 21:1-14

Then Paul answered, "What are you doing, weeping and breaking my heart? For I am ready not only to be imprisoned but even to die in Jerusalem for the name of the Lord Jesus." And since he would not be persuaded, we ceased and said, "Let the will of the Lord be done."
Acts 21:13-14

Finding and following God's will is one of the most important responsibilities of any Christian. Knowing what God wants, and then being willing to follow his will, is what discernment and discipleship are all about. Acts 21 paints a beautiful picture of a man who wanted to follow God's will in every way, even if it meant great personal sacrifice.

Paul had traveled extensively for a number of years sharing the message of the gospel and starting churches. At a certain point in his ministry, Paul felt "constrained by the Spirit" to go to Jerusalem (Acts 20:22-23). He didn't know exactly what would happen to him there "except that the Holy Spirit testifies to me in every city that imprisonment and afflictions await me."

Let's see if we have this straight. Paul made plans to travel to Jerusalem even though the Holy Spirit had made it clear that a prison cell and deep problems awaited him there. Why would a man do such a thing? Because he strongly believed that God was leading him to go. He was "constrained by the Spirit." He was so willing to obey

Finding and following God's will is one of the most important responsibilities of any Christian.

the Lord's will that he went even though it meant sacrifice. He was a man who was serious about knowing and doing God's will.

Notice the following important principles concerning the Lord's will. These principles apply to us today just as they did to Paul long ago.

The first principle about the Lord's will is that it can be challenging. Following God's will is not always easy; it is always right, but it isn't always easy. The first twelve verses of Acts 21 certainly remind us of that.

I can't help but think of career missionaries who leave family, friends, and conveniences when following God's will to serve in another land. That life can be challenging to say the least. I was recently with a group of missionaries serving in another nation. The level of poverty there was overwhelming. There were odd smells and unfamiliar foods, and the plumbing was not up to American standards. But they were called by God to go to this hard place and to share the good news with people who hadn't heard. They left behind the comforts of home that we take for granted. They missed family birthdays and special holidays. But they were following God's will.

Let's point out some of the different challenges Paul faced in following God's will. First, there was the emotional challenge. Verse one uses the words "when he had parted from them." This referred to Paul's dear friends, the Ephesian elders. These elders were godly men with whom he had prayed, served, and suffered. They were close friends, and he knew he would never see them again in this life. That was a tough goodbye. Acts 20:37 says, "There was much weeping on the part of all."

It was so hard to see my son-in-law, daughter, and granddaughter move away to Madagascar to become career missionaries. But I thought of how much harder it must have been for missionaries in earlier times. I can make video calls to my family on a regular basis and even visit them on occasion. Years ago, missionaries got on boats where it took months to reach their final destination. They could only send hand-written letters that may or may not reach family back home. And, they knew when they left that there was a strong possibility that they would never see their family again. Even though my challenge may not be as severe as earlier times, however, there is still an emotional challenge to following God's will today.

A second challenge was the physical challenge. Verses one and following tell us that Paul got on a ship and sailed from place to place on this journey to Jerusalem. That was hard enough. But often God's leading resulted in Paul taking long, exhausting journeys on foot. Following God's leading can lead to physical challenges today as well. I know a missionary who lost 30 pounds in three months due to the physical and medical difficulties of the region where he lived. In fact, all over the world, the demands of ministry can bring physical challenges.

A third challenge Paul faced as he followed God's will was the spiritual challenge. This may be the hardest challenge in following God's will. Our passage tells us that Paul's ship landed at a town called Tyre, where cargo was to be unloaded. There he met with the believers of that region and stayed for seven days. The Holy Spirit revealed to them the hardship Paul was going to suffer in Jerusalem, and they urged him not to go.

Even good people can urge you not to follow the Lord's will. Well-meaning friends and family don't want you to suffer the difficulties that may accompany God's plan. They may urge you to take the easier, safer road that leads away from a difficult path. I know missionaries whose families urged them not to go the mission field. God had clearly called them to go, but their families, even some Christian family members, plead-

Following God's will is always right, but it isn't always easy.

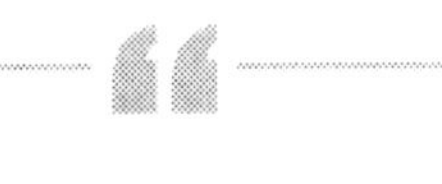

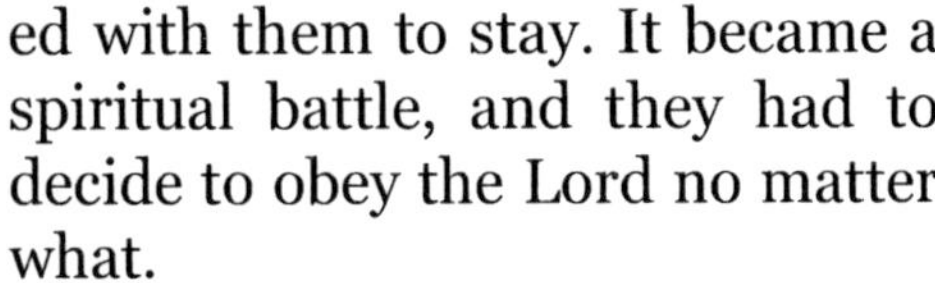

ed with them to stay. It became a spiritual battle, and they had to decide to obey the Lord no matter what.

The Lord's will should be cherished.

A good example of this spiritual battle is given to us in verses 7-12. A prophet named Agabus approached Paul, took Paul's belt, and bound Paul's feet and hands with it. Agabus told Paul that he was going to be bound in Jerusalem and handed over to the Gentiles. All of Paul's friends urged him to turn back. But Paul was absolutely determined to follow God's will no matter what.

That leads us to the second principle concerning God's will. The Lord's will should be cherished. Paul so desired to be faithful to God's will that nothing else mattered. He was more concerned about obeying the Lord than he was about comfort, freedom, or even his own life. He cherished the will of God more than he cherished ease, wealth, or power. He desired the will of God more than the wishes of his friends and companions. He wanted what God wanted.

Paul demonstrated that he cherished God's will by his actions. Paul did not equivocate. He stood firm by stating that he was going to obey God's clear leading to go to Jerusalem no matter what others said. In verse 13 he boldly declared, "I am ready not only to be imprisoned but even to die in Jerusalem for the name of the Lord Jesus." That was a man who believed that God's way is right and best even though it may also be difficult. That was a man who was serious about following God's will with all of his heart.

Another way Paul demonstrated that he cherished God's will was by his acceptance. Verse 14 records that Paul "would not be persuaded." That is, Paul was determined to follow the Lord, and no amount of tears or pleading from others would deter him. When they saw that, his friends ceased trying to talk him out of going to Jerusalem. In fact, they ended up saying what Paul had been saying all along, "Let the will of the Lord be done (v. 14)."

I started this chapter by saying that finding and following God's will is one of the most important responsibilities of any Christian. Finding and following his will matters deeply and eternally. Ask the Lord to show you his will for your life then follow it fully. God knows what we don't know, and he sees what we don't see—his purposes and plans are always best.

Food for Thought *Following God's will is challenging and difficult but it is always right and best. The right course of action for any Christian is to seek to know what God wants and then to follow God's way fully and completely. God has a plan and a purpose that is best for us even when it leads to difficulty and sacrifice. Obeying God's will is a believer's responsibility and joy.*

Faith in Action *Is there something that you know God wants you to do and you are hesitant to do it? Maybe it is a ministry he wants you to do in your local church. Maybe it is a conversation he wants you to have with a nonbeliever. Or, maybe he is calling you to something that requires deep sacrifice. Identify what that might be and follow Paul's example. Specifically, ask God to reveal his will to you and commit yourself to following his will for your life no matter the cost. Be willing to sacrifice as God calls you to sacrifice. Be willing to obey the Lord in every area of your life as he leads you.*

Prayer

Pray for the courage and the wisdom to follow God's leading even when he calls you to difficult things. Pray for those you know who are having a difficult time following God in every area of their lives. Pray for those around the world who are facing sacrifice and challenges because they are following the Lord's will.

The Dead Man Lives

Acts 25:13-27

When the accusers stood up, they brought no charge in his case of such evils as I supposed. Rather they had certain points of dispute with him about their own religion and about a certain Jesus, who was dead, but whom Paul asserted to be alive.
Acts 25:18-19

Legal shows are all the rage on television and movies. There are reality shows depicting people who are working through litigation before a judge and in courtrooms filled with cameras. There are dramas dealing with issues of justice and the law. It seems there is a great deal of interest in court cases and legal wrangling.

Paul certainly had his share of legal issues. After he followed the leadership of the Holy Spirit to go to Jerusalem, Paul was arrested just as he knew he would be. He was grabbed at the temple by an angry mob and beaten. The tempest drew the attention of the Roman soldiers who intervened and quieted the mob. Before they removed him, however, Paul used the opportunity to preach the message of the gospel to the crowd who had gathered. When he mentioned that he had been sent to take the message to the Gentiles, however, the shouting began all over again.

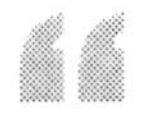

The resurrection of Jesus is at the very heart of the gospel message and the Christian faith.

Paul was whisked away by the Roman soldiers. They took him into custody and prepared to flog him in order to find out the meaning of the commotion surrounding him. Just before the flogging began, however, Paul mentioned to the centurion in charge that he was a Roman citizen. That changed everything. Roman citizens had legal rights. Thus began Paul's long journey through the complicated maze of the Roman legal system.

Paul first stood before the Jewish council where he created a split between the Pharisees and the Sadducees by mentioning his belief in the resurrection. That led to him being sent to the governor of the region, a man named Felix in Caesarea. Felix listened to Paul's testimony and the arguments of the Jews who stood against him. Somewhat perplexed by what to do, and hoping a bribe might come his way, Felix left Paul imprisoned until he was succeeded in office by a man named Festus.

Festus wrestled with the issues of the Jews and their case against Paul. Eventually, his unwillingness to deal with Paul in a just manner led Paul to appeal his case to Caesar. This appeal was always a part of the legal recourse for any Roman citizen. But, before Paul left for Rome, King Agrippa and his wife Bernice arrived in Caesarea. Festus asked for their legal advice on this vexing case concerning Paul, and they agreed to consider the case before Paul was sent on to Rome to make his appeal before Caesar.

When Festus summarized the case, he got it exactly right when he noted that the entire case revolved around "a certain Jesus, who was dead, but whom Paul asserted to be alive." The resurrection of Jesus was at the very core of the complicated legal issues facing Paul. It is also the central issue of the entire Christian faith. As the Bible teaches in 1 Corinthians 15:14, "If Christ has not been raised, then our preaching is in vain and your faith is in vain."

The resurrection of Jesus is at the very heart of the gospel message and the Christian faith. Let's note several things about the resurrection and its importance.

First, notice that the resurrection is central to the gospel. Not only was the resurrection central in the legal case of Paul, the resurrection was central to the preaching message of Paul. Everything rises or falls on the resurrection of Christ. Paul noted in 1 Corinthians 15:17, "If Christ has not been raised, your faith is futile and you are still in your sins."

Paul asserted that the resurrection is necessary to our forgiveness and salvation. Christ died to pay sin's debt. Christ rose to conquer sin's power. This is central to the case for faith made by Paul and the other New Testament writers. Jesus is alive and that demonstrates his power over sin, death, and hell.

Second, notice that the resurrection is controversial. Certainly Paul's insistence on the resurrection of Christ was a part of the controversy that had him in prison. The resurrection is still controversial in our world today. The gospel teaches that religion isn't enough and trying harder isn't sufficient. We are sinners who need a Savior who is greater than the power of our sin.

The resurrection points to the exclusive nature of faith. We need a risen Savior, not just sincerity or good works. I've watched Christian leaders being interviewed on secular television shows all of my life. Inevitably the questions seem to get to the exclusive claims of Christ. Is Jesus really the only way to heaven? Some Christian leaders have blinked under the secular pressure against such a narrow assertion. But others have stood strong under that same pressure with the claim Jesus made in John 14:6, "I am the way, and the truth, and the life. No one comes to the Father except through me."

We need a risen Savior who is greater than sin and who overcomes the grave.

Jesus makes the claim to be the only way to the Father because

Without the reality of the resurrection, we are still lost in our trespasses and sins.

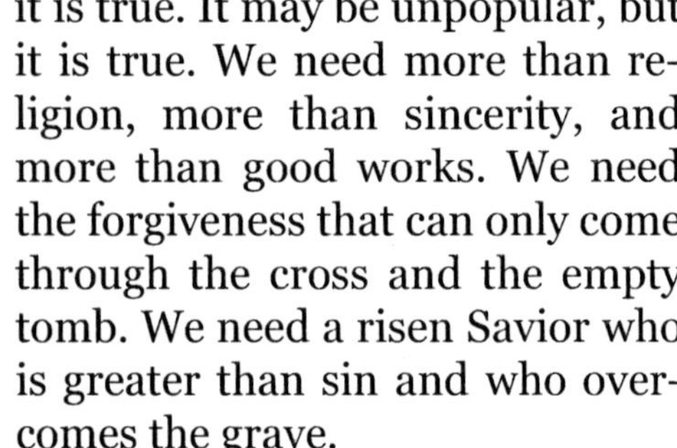

it is true. It may be unpopular, but it is true. We need more than religion, more than sincerity, and more than good works. We need the forgiveness that can only come through the cross and the empty tomb. We need a risen Savior who is greater than sin and who overcomes the grave.

Third, notice that the resurrection is consequential. Either Jesus is alive or he is not. Either he rose from the dead or he remains in the tomb. There are implications that follow the truth of what happened to Christ. If Jesus is alive, as the apostles' claimed and I believe, then he is Lord. If Jesus is Lord, then he is to be followed. If he is followed, then our lives will be changed forever.

For Paul, the resurrection of Christ meant his role as a Pharisee and all of his religious activities were not enough. It meant that his life was radically changed. It meant that he was willing to preach the gospel all over the Mediterranean region. It meant that he was willing to follow Jesus as he led him to Jerusalem and captivity. It meant that he was willing to live for Christ even though that resulted in living in a prison cell as he worked his way slowly through the Roman legal system. The resurrection had consequences for him.

Our belief in the resurrection has consequences for our lives as well. If we believe it to be true, it not only changes our eternity but it changes our here and now. It changes our actions, and it changes our attitudes. It changes our lives at every level because the resurrection is consequential.

Fourth, and finally, notice that the resurrection is converting. Paul was saved because Jesus rose from the dead. If you are child of God, it's because Jesus is alive. One of the basic tenets of faith is our belief that Jesus died and rose again. If he had only died on the cross but not risen from the grave, he would be the same as any other human religious leader. Without the reality of the resurrection, we are still lost in our trespasses and sins.

When I trusted Christ as my personal Savior, I was pretty young. But I knew that I was a sinner, and I knew that my sins had consequences. I remember the burden of guilt that I felt because of my sin. But knowing I was a sinner wasn't enough. I also acknowledged that there was a Savior who could do something about that sin. I didn't understand as a boy all that I would come to know later about Jesus, but I did know this: Jesus died for my sins on the cross, and he rose from the dead to overcome sin and death.

I placed my faith in the resurrected Jesus, and that made all the difference in my life. I found forgiveness of sin and purpose in life. I can live with victory over sin because Jesus lives. I am so thankful I discovered the power of this resurrected Savior in my own life. I hope you have discovered that same power in yours.

Food for Thought

Everything hinges on the resurrection of Jesus Christ. His resurrection means he has conquered the power of sin, death, and hell. It means he is Lord, and he is to be followed. It means our lives can be changed. It means we can be saved from our sins, we can have a home in heaven, and we can have hope in this world. It means that Jesus is worthy of any sacrifice we make and any service we give.

Faith in Action

Think through the amazing implications of the resurrection. Do you live with an awareness of the blessings of the resurrection? How would your life change if you lived out your belief that Christ is alive and has conquered sin? Read 1 Corinthians 15:57. The resurrection should give us hope and provide confidence for living a victorious and purposeful life. The resurrection leads us to surrender our lives to Jesus as Lord and Savior. Our belief in the resurrection should result in whole-heartedly following the Lord with every part of our lives.

Prayer

Praise and thank the Lord for the truth of the resurrection and the power that comes with that truth. Ask the Lord to give you a new boldness to stand for your faith. Ask the Lord to help you to live in victory and not defeat because of what he accomplished at the resurrection. Ask the Lord to help you to live your life with resurrection focus and resurrection power.

They All Became Encouraged

Acts 27:27-38

And when he had said these things he took bread, and giving thanks to God in the presence of all he broke it and began to eat. Then they all were encouraged and ate some food themselves.
Acts 27:35-36

Encouragement is greatest when times are darkest. Never is encouragement more needed and more beneficial than when it arrives on difficult days, and Paul knew something about difficult days.

Paul was sent to Rome because he had appealed to Caesar. So the authorities shipped him off to Rome where he awaited a court date. But the part where he was "shipped off to Rome" was rather complicated. There were no cars and no airplanes. Paul was put on a ship with some other prisoners and a group of soldiers led by a centurion named Julius. They were going to sail part of the way to Rome.

The journey began well enough. Julius treated Paul kindly, and he was even allowed to see friends at the frequent stops they made in various ports. But the winds proved difficult in the Mediterranean Sea on this trip, and each leg took longer than expected. As it grew later in the year, the dangers of travel on those treacherous waters

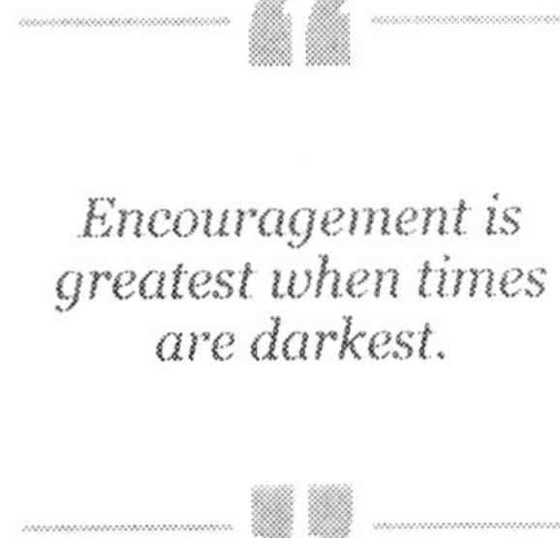

increased. Paul even warned the centurion that danger was coming with the trip. But the centurion was more persuaded by the captain of the ship than by the prisoner he was guarding. The soldiers and sailors decided to try to make it to Crete, where they would spend the winter until better sailing weather arrived.

The weather, however, refused to cooperate. The winds grew stronger and the waves higher. The ship was storm-tossed and buffeted by the waves and winds. The sky grew dark and the situation grave. Even the ships tackle was thrown overboard to lighten the load; such was the desperation of the hour. Sailors and soldiers alike began to lose hope.

Just as it must have seemed that all chance of survival was impossible, Paul spoke to the men. He reminded them of his earlier warning but then spoke of new hope. An angel had spoken to him in a vision and told him that the ship was going to be lost, but the lives of the men would be saved. Paul told the men that he had complete confidence that God would do exactly what he said. Yet, I imagine the men had doubts. They didn't know of a God who was greater than the weather, bigger than the seas, and more powerful than their problems. Could such a God exist?

This brings us to the story in today's verses. Here, we find five principles of discouragement and encouragement. First, notice that the discouraged can pray for daylight. In verses 27 and 28 we are told that at midnight the sailors began to suspect they were nearing land. Their long experience with the sea offered them a clue that they were in more shallow water. They tested and confirmed their theories; the water grew shallower with each sounding. But then they faced another danger. They feared they would hit the rocks and that the ship would be destroyed. Verse 29 tells us what these discouraged men did. They let down four anchors to stop the ship and "prayed for day to come." Have you ever been there? Have you ever faced such dark nights that all you could do was pray for the morning?

Some time ago I spoke to a woman in our church whose husband had passed away. I asked her how long it had been since his death, and she told me it had been almost a year. "I can't believe it has been that long," I said. "I can," she replied. That widow knew something about long nights when all she could do was pray for day to come. Perhaps you know something of that kind of discouragement as well.

Second, notice that the discouraged still have responsibilities. Some of the sailors decided to abandon the ship to make their own escape. Under the guise of lowering anchors, they began to lower the lifeboat instead. Instead of caring for others, they wanted to look out for themselves alone.

Paul spoke to the centurion and soldiers about what was taking place. In verse 31 he announced, "Unless these men stay in the ship, you cannot be saved." God had graciously promised to save all aboard the ship, but it was dependent upon them doing their responsibilities.

In an amazing act of faith in Paul and his vision, the soldiers cut away the ropes to the lifeboat and let it go. They would all live or die together. Perhaps they had been around Paul and his witness long enough to believe there might be something to this faith after all.

Third, notice that encouragers see the future. Dawn was near as the ship faced destruction on the rocks. But Paul was absolutely confident that the future was going to proceed just as the angel of the Lord had promised. His belief in the future God promised allowed him to encourage his fellow passengers in an amazing way. Two weeks had passed since the storm broke. The passengers had been unable to eat because of their con-

We may not know all the details of our future, but we know we can count on the Lord as we face that future.

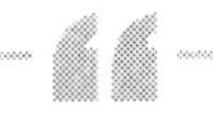

Thanksgiving is at the heart of the life of an encourager.

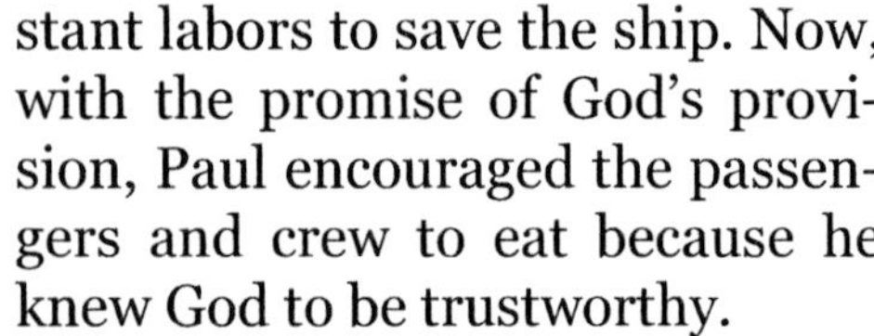

stant labors to save the ship. Now, with the promise of God's provision, Paul encouraged the passengers and crew to eat because he knew God to be trustworthy.

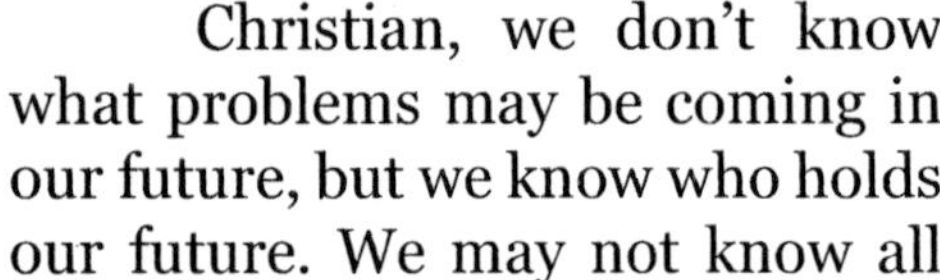

Christian, we don't know what problems may be coming in our future, but we know who holds our future. We may not know all the details of our future, but we know we can count on the Lord as we face that future. That truth gives us great confidence and provides tremendous encouragement to us.

Fourth, notice that encouragers are thankful for small blessings. Perhaps no other single trait clearly separates those who encourage from those who don't. Thanksgiving is at the heart of the life of an encourager. An encourager knows there is much for which to be grateful.

Verse 35 tells us that Paul took bread, gave thanks to God for it, broke it, and then began to eat. Verse 36 records the reaction. "Then they all were encouraged and ate some food themselves." Bread is such a small thing to us. But when you haven't eaten for two weeks, you realize how great bread tastes. That group of sailors faced a new appreciation for bread and a new hope for the future. They were encouraged.

Fifth, and finally, notice that encouragers prepare for tomorrow. When they had all eaten, they lightened the ship by throwing the rest of the wheat into the sea as they waited for daylight. In other words, they prepared for the next day and the promise that came with it. With renewed thanksgiving for God's provision in the past, they prepared for tomorrow.

Encouragers know the blessings of yesterday are reminders of the promises for tomorrow. We can trust God with our future. Just as he has been trustworthy with our past, he will be trustworthy with our future. What an encouraging thought! By the way, the story ends just as God promised. All 276 people on board that ship were saved—God kept his promise.

Encouragers know the blessings of yesterday are reminders of the promises for tomorrow.

I want to encourage you today. You may be facing some overwhelming problems. But let me remind you that you have a great Savior. Let me urge you to remember that God will keep his promise to be with us today, and he will keep his promise to take us to be with him some day. We can be encouraged because God's truth always lifts up our souls!

Food for Thought

Encouragement is greatest when times are darkest. We can find encouragement even in our most difficult days, because we can trust God's presence and his promises. And God allows us to encourage others through the difficulties and struggles of life. Perhaps God wants to use you to encourage someone who is going through the storms of life right now.

Faith in Action

Are you or someone you know in the middle of discouragement right now? Did this story encourage your heart today? Reflect on a time in the past where God kept his promise to provide for you or protect you. Count your blessings! Now, apply the reality of God's promise kept in the past to your situation right now. Allow that to encourage your heart. Then, find a way to be an encourager to others today. Remind others that God can be counted on no matter what storms may come. Proclaim to them that God is trustworthy. Encourage them by showing them the blessings God has provided even in the midst of the storm. Our testimony to the gospel is never stronger than when we can share it on difficult days.

Prayer

Ask the Lord to encourage you where you need it. And, ask the Lord to help you to be an encourager to others. Ask the Lord to help you recognize the many blessings he has provided and to help you to trust the promises he has made. And ask him to provide you with opportunities to encourage others who are facing times of discouragement.

Some Were Persuaded

Acts 28:17-31

From morning till evening he expounded to them, testifying to the kingdom of God and trying to convince them about Jesus both from the Law of Moses and from the Prophets. And some were convinced by what he said, but others disbelieved.
Acts 28:23-24

Throughout the chapters of the book of Acts we have seen the bold witness of the early church. There was enthusiasm for the Lord's work in their own lives, but there was also a passion to share the Lord's work with others. This passion is clearly demonstrated in the last chapter of this great book of the Bible.

Paul, after a long, harrowing journey that included being shipwrecked, finally arrived in Rome to stand before Caesar. But the machinery of the Roman legal system worked slowly, so Paul was given a good deal of freedom; only one soldier guarded Paul. Paul was allowed to stay by himself and continue to witness to his faith in the Lord Jesus Christ.

We can learn several valuable lessons from the witness of Paul during this two-year period of confinement while he awaited trial. Each of these lessons is valuable to

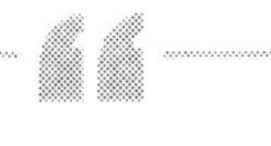

Witnesses look for opportunities everywhere.

any who want the same passion and effectiveness as demonstrated by the early church.

The first lesson taught in this passage is that witnesses look for opportunities everywhere. After Paul arrived at Rome, he followed his customary pattern of sharing the gospel first with the Jews. He called together the leaders of the Jews in Rome, and they gathered to hear him. He told them the story of his accusers, his imprisonment, his appeal to Caesar, and of course, of the message of Jesus.

I wonder what we would have done had we been in Paul's situation? Would we have complained about the terrible situation in which we found ourselves? Is it possible that we would have been sulking about our undeserved captivity or fretting about our upcoming trial before Caesar? I wonder if I would have looked for opportunities to share the message of the gospel with those around me?

There was something amazing about these early Christians. Circumstances did not change their obedience, and problems did not dampen their enthusiasm for the gospel. Perhaps that is why God used them so powerfully to change the world.

The second lesson this passage teaches is that witnesses share the message faithfully. Verse 23 tells us that the Jewish leaders came back with a larger group some days later. The witness Paul gave to those leaders was instructive and continuous. The Bible tells us that he shared "from morning till evening." He preached and witnessed to them all day long.

I was in Cuba a few years ago speaking to a gathering of about 130 pastors. They gathered to listen for hours on end. All morning they listened intently as another American pastor and I spoke to them. They broke for lunch and played baseball for an hour. After lunch they gathered and listened again all afternoon. Then, after a small supper, they listened intently to another session all evening. I'm not sure that an American audience would listen so carefully or for so long a time.

The witness Paul gave was direct. Our key verse says, "He expounded to them, testifying to the kingdom of God." He got to the heart of God's message to mankind. He told them the truth about sin, righteousness, and judgment. He spoke to them of grace, love, and forgiveness. He showed them God's eternal plan and purpose. I love the direct nature of the witness of the early church. They did not beat around the bush. They told the truth, the whole truth, and nothing but the truth.

The witness Paul gave was passionate. Paul wanted to persuade the Jewish leaders to follow Christ. The Bible tells us he was "trying to convince them." While we cannot make others follow Christ, we certainly desire that they would. The early church urged, persuaded, argued, and encouraged. They were not neutral on the issue of whether others should be saved. They were passionate in their desire to see others find the same salvation they had discovered.

The witness Paul gave was personal. Verse 23 says he was trying to convince them "about Jesus." The witness of the early church was always directed towards the person and work of Jesus. He is the one who saves, and he is the only hope for every person. The gospel is personal. It is about Jesus and how we can have a personal relationship with God through the work of this great Savior.

Paul's witness was contextual. We are told that Paul was trying to convince them about Jesus "both from the Law of Moses and from the Prophets." These Jewish leaders knew the Law and the Prophets, and Paul showed them how Jesus was the fulfillment of the Law and the promise of the Prophets. He started with what they knew and pointed them to Jesus.

> *"Circumstances did not change their obedience, and problems did not dampen their enthusiasm for the gospel."*

All we can do is share the message of the gospel with passion and accuracy—we cannot determine outcomes.

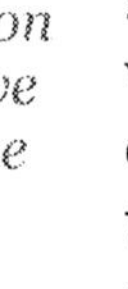

The third lesson to be learned from this passage is that witnesses know that responses vary. Verse 24 notes that "some were convinced by what he said, but others disbelieved." All we can do is share the message of the gospel with passion and accuracy—we cannot determine outcomes. Some will hear the message of the gospel, repent, and believe. Others will hear that same message, ignore it, and reject it. The early church saw plenty of both responses. Sometimes there were periods of great harvest; at other times there were very few converts. But the early church remained faithful to share the message as clearly and passionately as they could, regardless of the response.

The fourth lesson taught by this passage is that God blesses the faithful proclamation of the gospel. The last two verses of the book of Acts tell us that Paul remained in Rome for two years awaiting trial. We are told neither the end results of the trial nor the ending of Paul's life. Rather, the book ends by telling us of Paul's faithful witness in Rome. He welcomed all who visited him as he proclaimed and taught about the Lord Jesus Christ "with all boldness and without hindrance." God continued to bless Paul's proclamation of his word, even while he was in captivity in Rome. The truth continued to be proclaimed. Not even the power of Rome could hinder the work of God.

God is at work in our day, too. The work continues despite all of the problems and difficulties in this fallen world. He is working, and neither the powers of this world nor hell itself can hinder that work. The amazing, incredible thing God does is work through faithful witnesses like you and me. What a blessing to know and serve our great God!

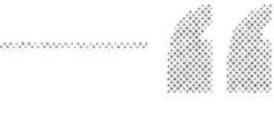

God is working, and neither the powers of this world nor hell itself can hinder that work.

Food for Thought

God has always worked through faithful witnesses who share the message of the gospel. When we faithfully share the message of the gospel, we can be used by God to make a lasting difference in this world and in eternity. We can be faithful in our witness for God despite the circumstances or problems that we face. Like the early church believers, we can be bold and effective witnesses of the gospel message.

Faith in Action

Today is the last day of your 30-day study of Acts. Look back over the last few weeks and identify the truths that God has revealed to you, the places in your heart where the Spirit has convicted you, and the things in your life that God wants you to do or change. Write them down in this book as a testimony of where God is working in your life. As you document this testimony, let the evidence of God's work in your life challenge you and excite you. He has a plan and purpose for your life, and he wants to use you to make an impact in your world.

Prayer

Thank the Lord for all that he has taught you and shown you through your study of Acts. Pray over each of the things you wrote down in the Action Step, and ask God for help to apply these lessons to your life. Ask the Lord to inspire you and your church to be like the early church with a passion for the things of God and a greater boldness in your witness.

Finding L.I.F.E. in Jesus!

Everyone wants to be happy. The hard part is determining exactly what that means. For some, happiness is defined through relationships. They believe that popularity, a huge friend list on Facebook, and a significant other produces happiness. For others, happiness is defined through success. They believe that personal achievement, a huge number in their bank account, and plenty of expensive toys produces happiness. For still others, happiness is defined through community. They believe that personal growth, a huge impact for societal change, and embracing diversity produces happiness. And these things do—until they don't.

Experiencing happiness is as difficult as catching the greased pig at the county fair. It appears to be right in front of us, but then it slips through our fingers and is gone. Friends, achievement, and personal growth have the potential to bring happiness into our lives, but when our friends disappear, success eludes us, and we realize that we're incapable of self-transformation, happiness is quickly replaced by disillusionment and depression. The problem with pursuing happiness is that it is an emotion that is driven by our circumstances. And let's be honest—we all tend to have more negative than positive experiences in our lives.

So, what's the answer? Should we keep doing the same things while expecting different results, or should we consider what Jesus has to say about finding our purpose for life? If you want to stay on the hamster wheel while you try to catch up to happiness, you can stop reading here. But if you're ready to consider what God wants to do in your life, please read on.

God never promises happiness in the Bible. Are you surprised to hear that? Instead, he promises something much greater—joy. While happiness is an emotion fueled by circumstance, joy is an attitude fueled by God's Spirit. Happiness is self-determined. In other words, I am the sole determiner of whether I'm happy at any given moment. Joy, on the other hand, is God-determined. God has promised to give us joy, and it isn't based on our circumstances—it's based on God's character and promises.

This is why Jesus never talks about giving people happiness. He knew all too well that chasing happiness is like chasing your shadow. You can never catch it. Instead, he talks about giving people life. He said, "I came that they may have life and have it abundantly (Jn 10:10)." Here, Jesus reveals that the thing people really want, whether they know it or not, is abundant life. To have an abundant life means that you are personally satisfied in all areas of your life, and you experience peace and contentment as a result. Jesus' statement also means that we do not have the capacity to create that kind of life for ourselves. Jesus came in order to give it to us. But how? The Bible tells us that achieving this kind of satisfied life requires us to know something about God, ourselves, and the reason for the death and resurrection of Jesus Christ.

First, we must understand God's **love**. The Bible says that God is love (I Jn 4:8), and God created us so that we could know him and experience his love (Gen 1:26-31). God created us to be worshipers and to live forever in the reality of his glory. And, when sin marred his perfect creation, he created a plan to free men and women from its curse. At just the right time in history, God sent his own Son, Jesus, into our world. "For God so loved the world, that he gave his only Son, that whoever believes in him should not perish but have eternal life (Jn

3:16).” It is God’s love that motivates him to restore relationship with those who are separated from him by sin.

Second, we must understand our **isolation**. To be isolated is to be separated from someone, and as a result, to be alone. This is what sin has done to us. It has separated us from the very one we were created to know, love, and worship—God. When Adam and Eve rebelled against God by breaking the lone command he had given them, the entire world was brought under the curse of sin (Gen 3). As a result, God removed them from the Garden of Eden, and their perfect fellowship with God was broken. In an instant, they had become isolated from God because of their sin. From that moment to this, every person born into this world is guilty of sin. The Bible says, “For all have sinned and fall short of the glory of God (Rom 3:23).” Because of this “there is none righteous, no, not one (Rom 3:10).” Further, “The wages of sin is death (Rom 6:23a).” We were created to love and worship God in perfect community, but now because of sin we are isolated from him. Meanwhile, we try to satisfy this desire to know God by pursuing our own happiness, even though we can never hope to attain it. And in doing so, we risk being isolated from God for all eternity.

Third, we must understand our need for **forgiveness.** There is only one way to experience God’s love and escape the isolation caused by sin—we must experience God’s forgiveness. In spite of sin, God never stopped loving the people he created. He promised Adam and Eve that he would send someone who could fix the problem they had created. When it was time, God sent his own Son, Jesus, to be the world’s Savior. This, too, was an act of God’s love. The Bible says, “God shows his love for us in that while we were still sinners, Christ died for us (Rom 5:8).” When Jesus died on the cross, he was paying the penalty for our sins (Rom 3:23-26). When God raised Jesus from the dead, it was to demonstrate that forgiveness was available to all who would receive it by faith. Paul explains how this happens in his letter to the Ephesians. "For by grace you have been saved through faith. And this is not your own doing; it is the gift of God, not a result of works, so that no one may boast (Eph 2:8-9)."

The reality is that we cannot experience salvation as a result of our own efforts. We can try to be a good person, go to a church, even give a ton of money to worthy causes—none of these "works" can provide forgiveness. No matter how hard we try, we will always "fall short of the glory of God." That is why we must receive God's offer of forgiveness and salvation by faith. Faith simply means to trust or believe. Salvation requires us to believe that God loves us, that we are isolated from him by our sins, and that his Son Jesus died and was raised to life again to pay the sin debt that we owe God because of our sins. When we take God up on his offer of the gift of salvation, he doesn't just give us forgiveness—he gives us life! The Bible says, "The free gift of God is eternal life in Christ Jesus our Lord (Rom 6:23)."

Fourth, we must understand the **enjoyment** that comes from knowing, loving, and worshiping God. Whether we know it or not, we are slaves to sin until God sets us free (Rom 6:20-23). This was the ultimate reason that God sent his Son, Jesus, to die on the cross for our sins—God sent Jesus so that we could be set free from our sins. Jesus said, "You will know the truth, and the truth will set you free. . . . Everyone who commits sin is a slave to sin. . . . So, if the Son sets you free, you will be free indeed (Jn 8:32-36)." Jesus was teaching us that we must be set free from sin in order to enjoy the life that God has given us—both now and in eternity future. We are set free when we commit our lives to Jesus Christ through faith in his death and resurrection. Then, and only then, will we find joy in the abundant life of Jesus Christ!

So, the question for you is a simple one: Are you ready to experience freedom from sin and the abundant life that Jesus promised you? If so, God is waiting for to talk with him about it (Jer 29:13). Stop right where you are and make this your prayer to God,

"Father in heaven, I know that I'm a sinner. I know that I've done lots of things that displease you and disappoint you. And, I know that I'm isolated from you because of my sin. I know that if I die without knowing you, I will spend forever separated from you in hell. But, I believe that Jesus is your sinless Son, and I believe that he died on the cross for me. I believe that he died to provide a perfect payment for my sin debt. I believe that you raised him from the dead so that I could experience forgiveness for my sins. Right now, Father, I'm asking you to forgive me of my sins and save me. I am receiving your Son Jesus as my personal Lord and Savior. I will follow you the rest of my life. Please give me the joy of a life spent knowing, loving, and worshiping you. I ask these things in Jesus' name, Amen."

If you made the decision to accept Jesus as your Savior today, we want to talk with you! Please contact the people at www.seed-publishing-group.com. We would love to talk with you about your decision and help you with your first steps in following Jesus!